Kindergarten-
1st Grade

Show What You Know™

Ohio Proficiency Test Preparation

Written By:
Andrea Karch Balas MS, MA
Judy Cafmeyer

Illustrated By:
Joseph Humphries

05 04 03 02 01 20 19 18 17 16 15 14 13 12 11 10 9 8 7 6 5 4 3

ISBN 1-884183-37-9

Limit of Liability/Disclaimer of Warranty: The authors and publishers have used their best efforts in preparing this book. Englefield and Arnold, Inc. and the authors make no representation or warranties with respect to the contents of this book and specifically disclaim any implied warranties and shall in no event be liable for any loss of any kind including but not limited to special, incidental, consequential, or other damages.

Englefield and Arnold, Inc. P.O. Box 341348, 6344 Nicholas Drive, Columbus, OH 43234-1348
1-877-PASSING (727-7464) • (614) 764-1211 • Fax: (614) 764-1311
webpage: www.eapublishing.com

Acknowledgements

Englefield and Arnold Publishing acknowledges the following for their efforts in making this proficiency material available for Ohio students, parents, and teachers:

Cindi Englefield Arnold, President/Publisher
Eloise Boehm-Sasala, Vice President/Managing Editor
Mercedes Baltzell, Associate Editor
Joseph Humphries, Illustrator/Cover Designer

About the Authors:

Andrea Karch Balas, MS, MA, is an educator and a scientist who has taught both in the traditional classroom and in nonformal educational settings, from kindergarten to adult. Andrea has presented nationally and internationally her research on the teaching and learning of science, including integrating science into all subject areas of school curriculum. She is currently supervising student teachers in a Masters of Education program, and is a doctoral candidate at The Ohio State University.

Judy Cafmeyer has taught for seventeen years in public and private schools from kindergarten to eighth grade. She is currently a proficiency workshop presenter and educational author for Englefield and Arnold Publishing, and is a reporter for *the Ohio Proficiency Press*. A graduate of The Ohio State University with a degree in elementary education, Judy has experienced education from various vantage points: as a teacher, on district curriculum committees, as a parent, a volunteer, and as a school board officer.

Teacher Reviewers:
Tonya Hawk
Sara Keaney
Mary Sasala

Circle Question Paddle Pattern

The open and filled circles will be used over and over again, particularly for the circle questions found under each lesson. It is recommended that these circles be mounted on heavier paper and laminated for durability. Create one paddle by attaching the two circles to a craft stick, back-to-back. The paddle presents a closed circle on one side and an open circle on the other side. Students will become familiar with the idea that a filled circle represents an answer choice (i.e., on the Ohio proficiency test, a multiple choice question is answered by completely filling in a circle).

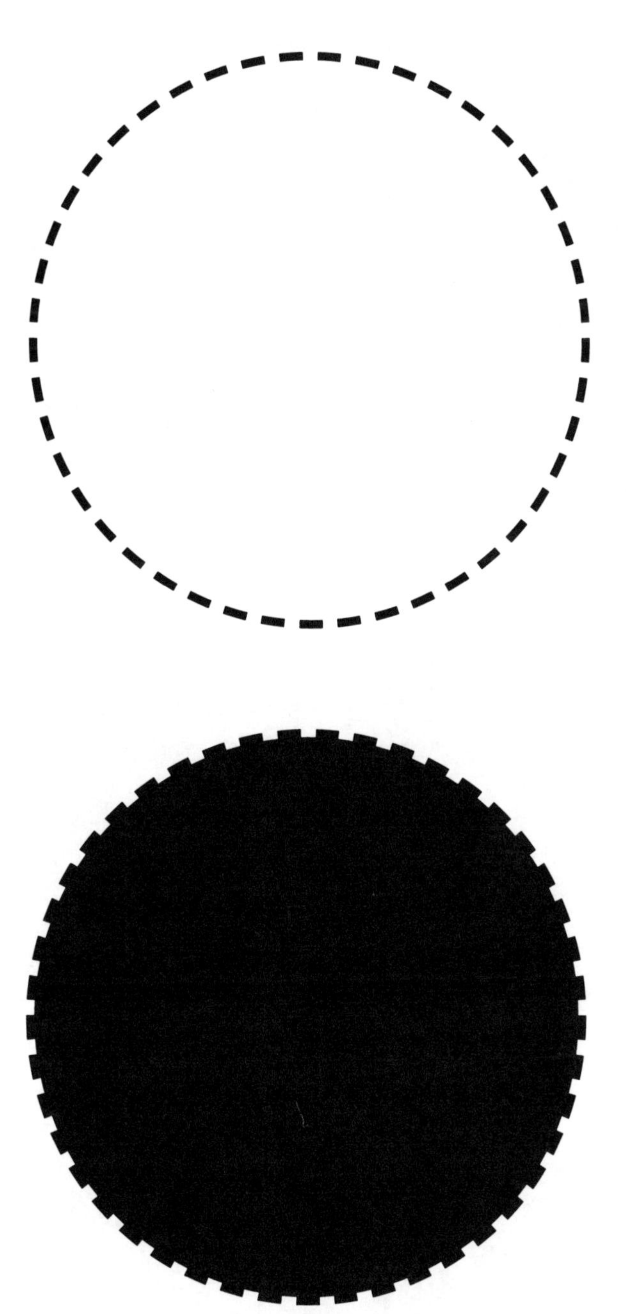

Follow Directions

Use a red crayon to color:

- the apple with a leaf.
- the smallest apple.
- the group of two apples.
- the apple with a worm.

Use a yellow crayon to color:

- the apple slices.
- the apple with no stem or leaf.
- the apple core.

Use a green crayon to color:

- the apple with the bite taken out of it.
- the apple with a stem but no leaf.

Graph the apples from activity A1 by color.

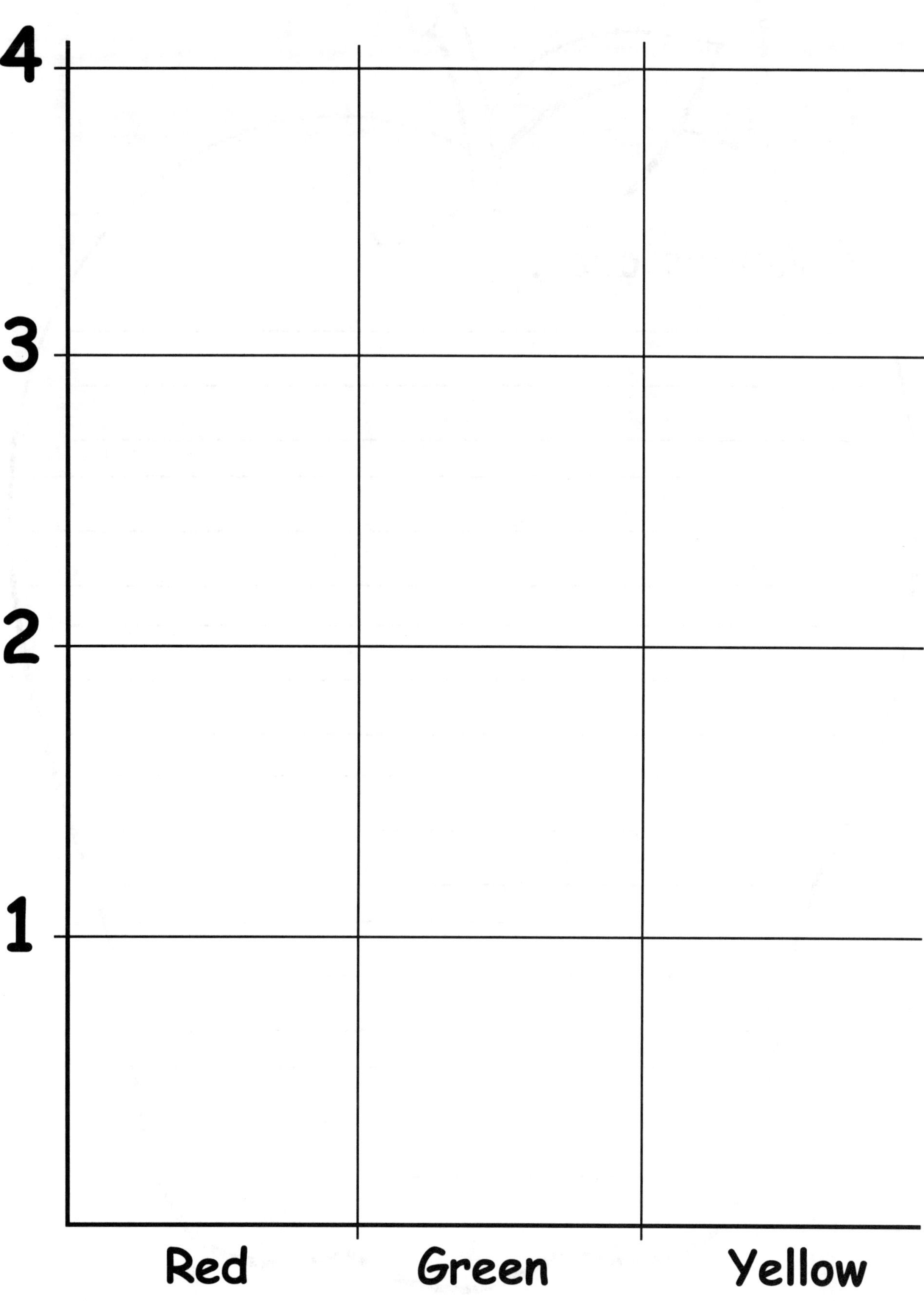

Complete the prompt.

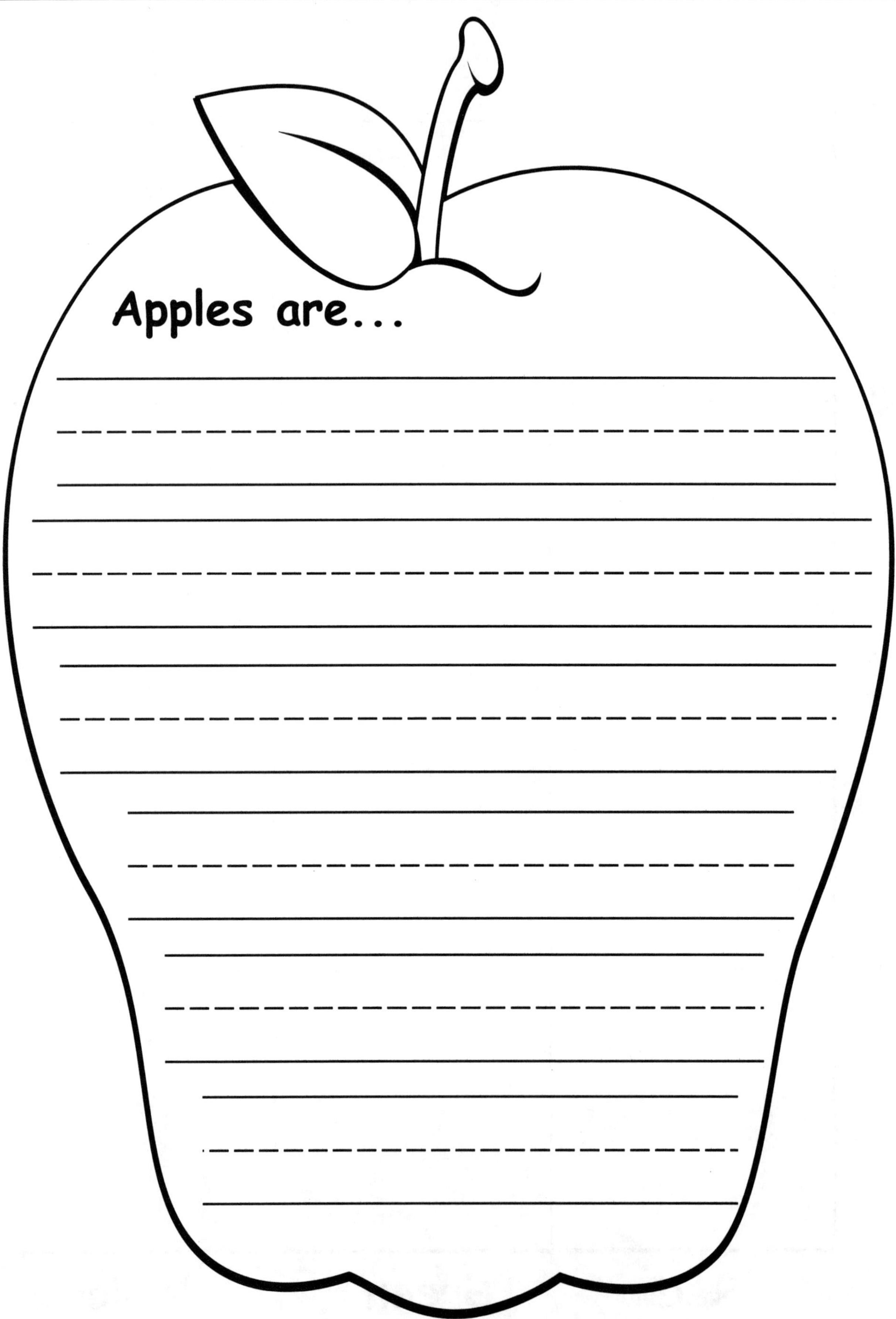

Fill in the circles for the items with the same beginning sound as the word **butter.**

Look at the pictures of the butter making sequence. Color the pictures. Write in the missing numbers to put the pictures of how butter is made in the correct order. Complete the sequence by drawing a picture of someone using butter in the fifth square.

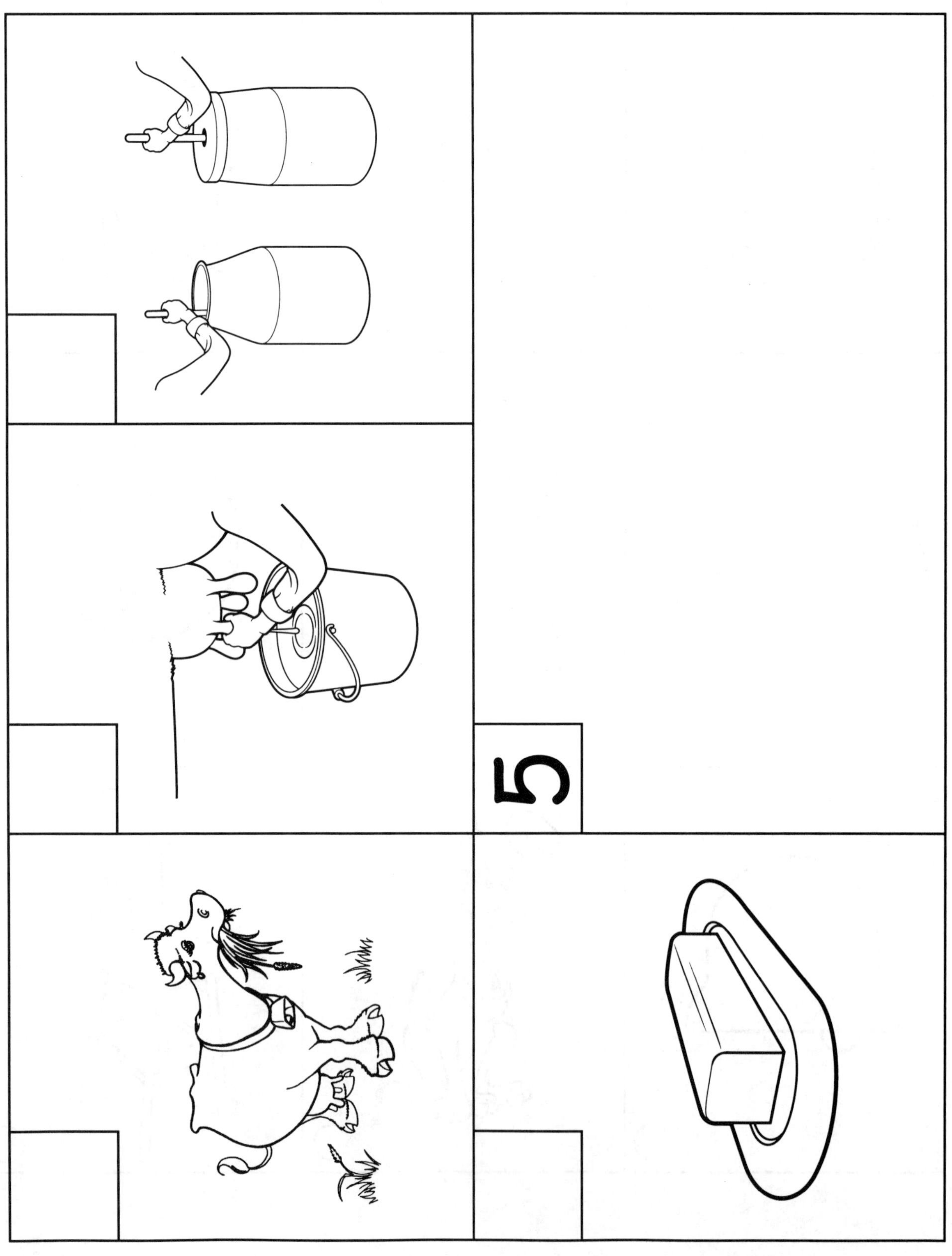

Fill in the circle to select each answer choice.

It's neat to eat...	Yes	No
1. butter blobs	○	○
2. butterflies	○	○
3. boxes	○	○
4. bottles	○	○
5. peanut butter	○	○
6. mushrooms	○	○
7. berries	○	○
8. bagels	○	○
9. bicycles	○	○
10. balloons	○	○

- Color the sandbox brown.
- Color the school house red.
- Color the swing set yellow.
- Color the leaves on the trees green.
- Color the trunks of the trees brown.
- Color the flagpole black.

Mark a black X in the spot where you would bury a treasure.

1. Trace the rivers with a blue crayon.
2. Locate the capital city of Ohio. Draw a flag near it.
3. Find Lake Erie. Draw a boat on the lake.
4. Can you find the area of the state where your school is located? Mark this area with a green X.

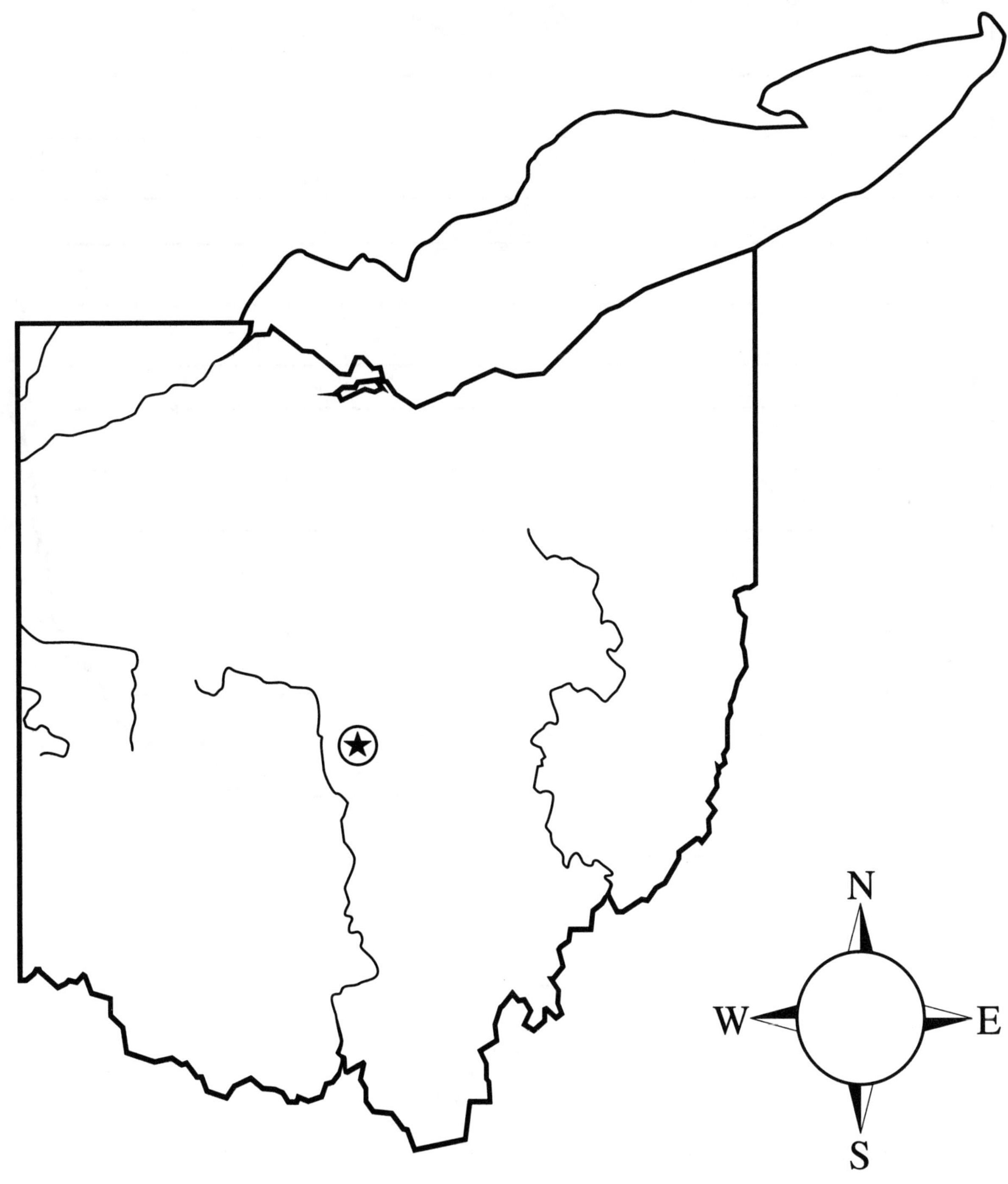

Complete the prompt.

Complete the prompt.

As dandelion seeds fly in the air...

Take a poll of the class. How many boys have "given" or "not given" someone a dandelion bouquet? Write the number for each category, then fill in the correct number of circles. Repeat.

Boys

Given ______

○ ○ ○ ○ ○ ○
○ ○ ○ ○ ○ ○
○ ○ ○ ○ ○ ○
○ ○ ○ ○ ○ ○

Not Given ______

○ ○ ○ ○ ○ ○
○ ○ ○ ○ ○ ○
○ ○ ○ ○ ○ ○
○ ○ ○ ○ ○ ○

Girls

Given ______

○ ○ ○ ○ ○ ○
○ ○ ○ ○ ○ ○
○ ○ ○ ○ ○ ○
○ ○ ○ ○ ○ ○

Not Given ______

○ ○ ○ ○ ○ ○
○ ○ ○ ○ ○ ○
○ ○ ○ ○ ○ ○
○ ○ ○ ○ ○ ○

Boys and Girls

Given ______

○ ○ ○ ○ ○ ○
○ ○ ○ ○ ○ ○
○ ○ ○ ○ ○ ○
○ ○ ○ ○ ○ ○

Not Given ______

○ ○ ○ ○ ○ ○
○ ○ ○ ○ ○ ○
○ ○ ○ ○ ○ ○
○ ○ ○ ○ ○ ○

The life cycle of a dandelion.

Color the six pictures, then cut them out. Glue the pictures on the top half of the page in the correct sequence.

1	2	3
4	5	6

Fill in the circle to identify each item as living or nonliving.

	Living	Nonliving
1. money	○	○
2. ice cream cone	○	○
3. child	○	○
4. hat	○	○
5. sock	○	○
6. car	○	○
7. kitten	○	○
8. baseball	○	○
9. rocks	○	○
10. caterpillar	○	○

Fun Facts About My Face! Complete each sentence.

I have ______________________ hair.

I have ______________________ eyes.

I have ______________________ nose.

I have ______________________ ears.

I have ____________ ____________ .

Fill in the circles for the items with the same beginning sound as the word **fact.**

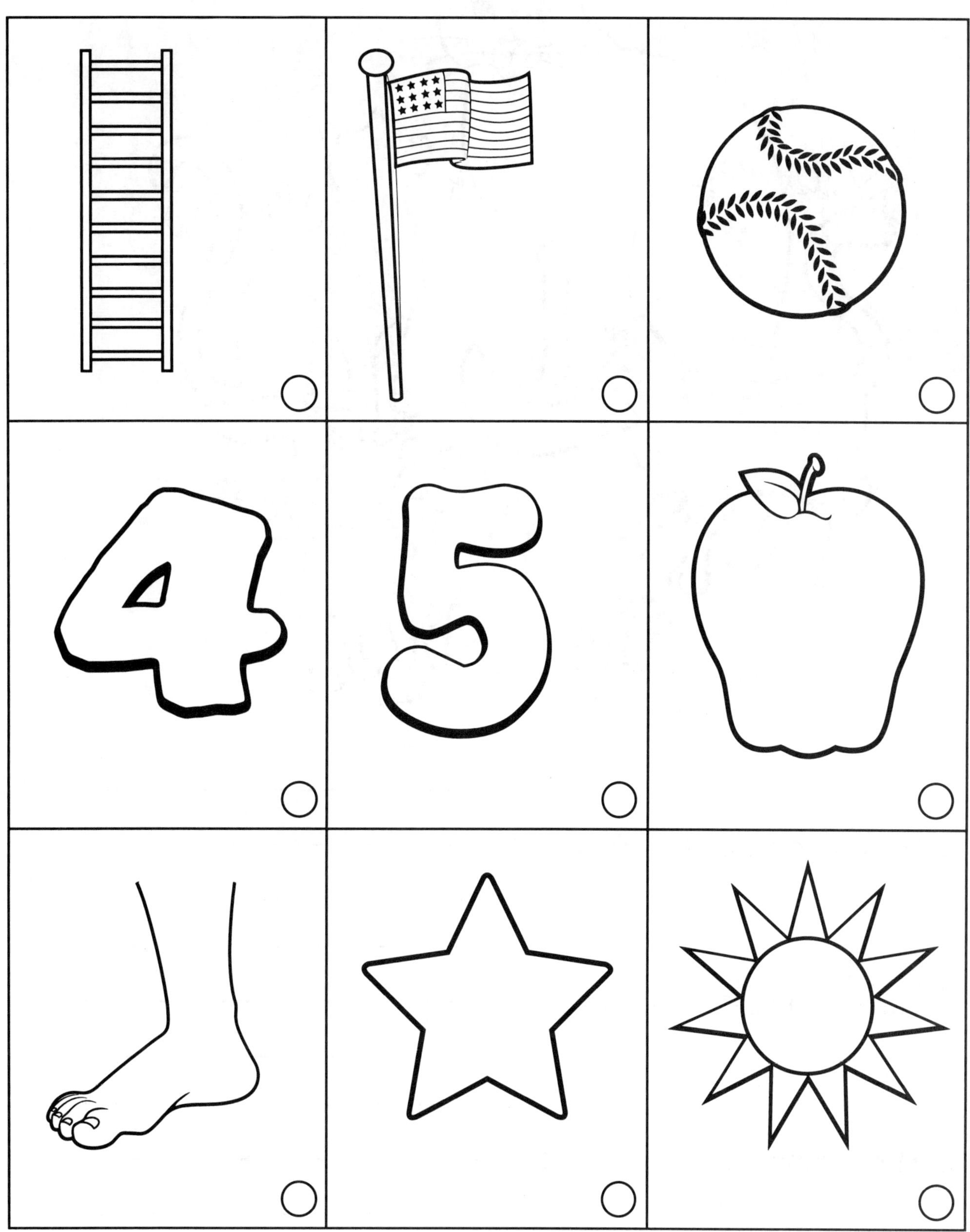

Color the biggest cat in the group yellow.

1. How many cats are pictured?

2. How many cats have stripes?

3. How many ears do you see?

Color the smallest dog in the group brown.

1. How many dogs are pictured? ____________________

2. How many dogs have a bone? ____________________

3. How many tails do you see? ____________________

Color the number of squares on the graph to show the height of each character.

---

3 feet | 4 feet | 2 feet | 1 foot

5 feet tall				
4 feet tall				
3 feet tall				
2 feet tall				
1 foot tall				
	boy	girl	dog	rabbit

Today is

Today's Weather

Draw a symbol for each month of the year.

The Months of the Year

January	February	March	April	May	June
July	August	September	October	November	December

Circle the correct answer in relation to today's date.

1. Today is:	Sunday	Monday	Tuesday	Wednesday	Thursday	Friday	Saturday
2. Tomorrow is:	Sunday	Monday	Tuesday	Wednesday	Thursday	Friday	Saturday
3. Yesterday was:	Sunday	Monday	Tuesday	Wednesday	Thursday	Friday	Saturday
4. This month is:	January	February	March	April	May	June	
	July	August	September	October	November	December	
5. Next month is:	January	February	March	April	May	June	
	July	August	September	October	November	December	
6. Last month was:	January	February	March	April	May	June	
	July	August	September	October	November	December	
7. The time right now is:	a.m.	p.m.					

Carefully cut out each item along the dotted lines. Use each to measure different objects around the classroom.

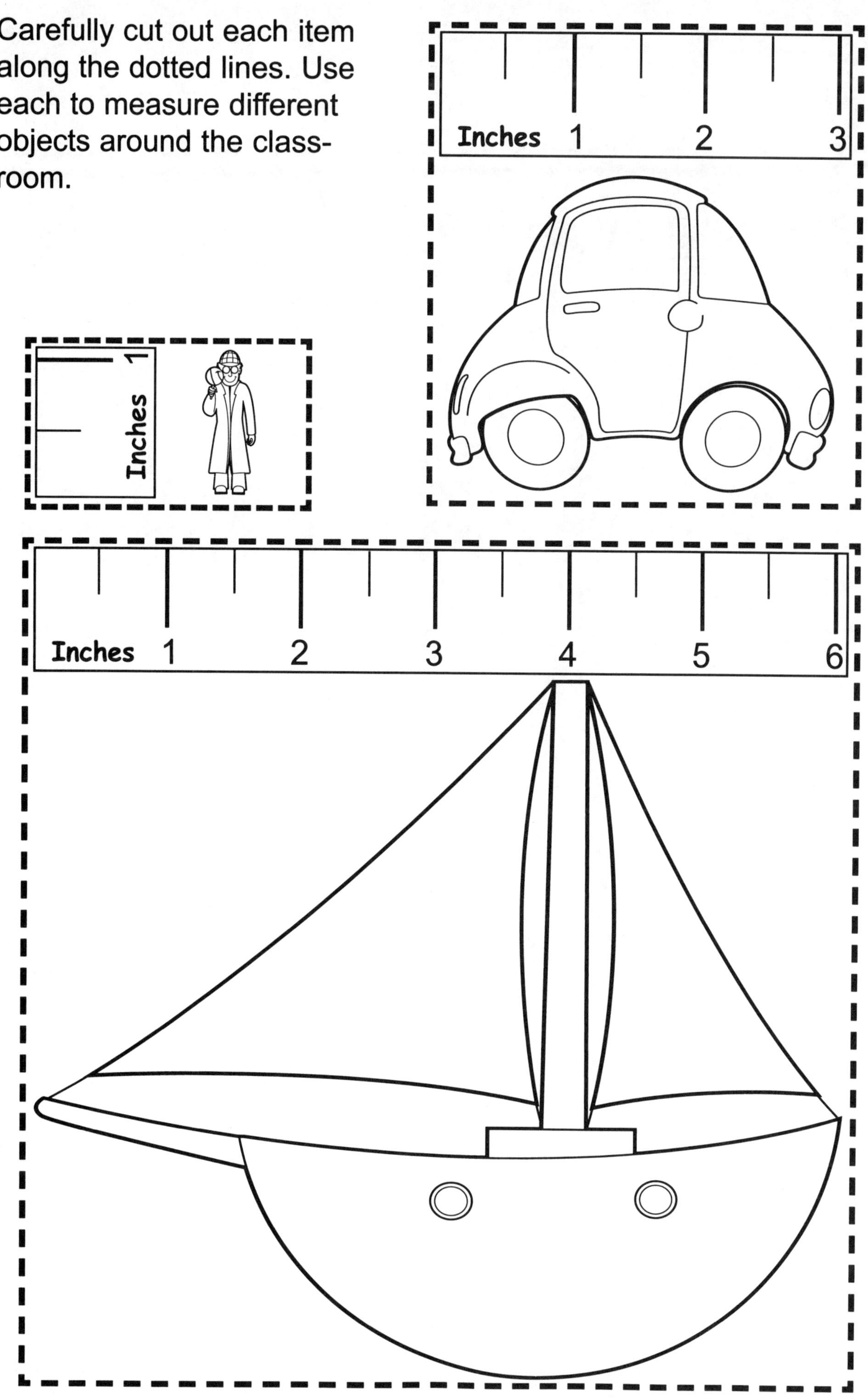

Inspector Inch and his vehicles from activity **I1** will be used to measure items in the classroom. How many lengths of Inspector Inch does it take to completely measure the width of your desk? Record the measure. How many lengths of Inspector Inch's three-inch car does it take to completely measure the width of the desk? Record that number. Follow the same directions using the boat. Record those numbers.

Measure and Compare	**Inspector Inch** 1 inch	**Inspector Inch's Car** 3 inches	**Inspector Inch's Boat** 6 inches
book			
desk			

Using Inspector Inch, determine if the items below are greater than (>) or less than (<) one inch in size.

	Larger than Inspector Inch >	Smaller than Inspector Inch <
pencil	○	○
your fingernail	○	○
paper clip	○	○
your thumb	○	○
building block	○	○
glue bottle	○	○
crayon	○	○

Write a short story in which you are the main character. Draw a picture for your story.

Learn more about yourself and others by answering each of these questions.

	Yes	No
1. I am a boy.	○	○
2. I am a girl.	○	○
3. I have a brother.	○	○
4. I have a sister.	○	○
5. I have a pet.	○	○
6. I ride the bus to school.	○	○

Take a class poll. Fill in the circles to show the total number of yes responses to each sentence. Write the total in the box.

1. I am a boy.

2. I am a girl.

3. I have a brother.

4. I have a sister.

5. I have a pet.

6. I ride the bus to school.

Fill in the circle to indicate which keyhole matches the shape on each key.

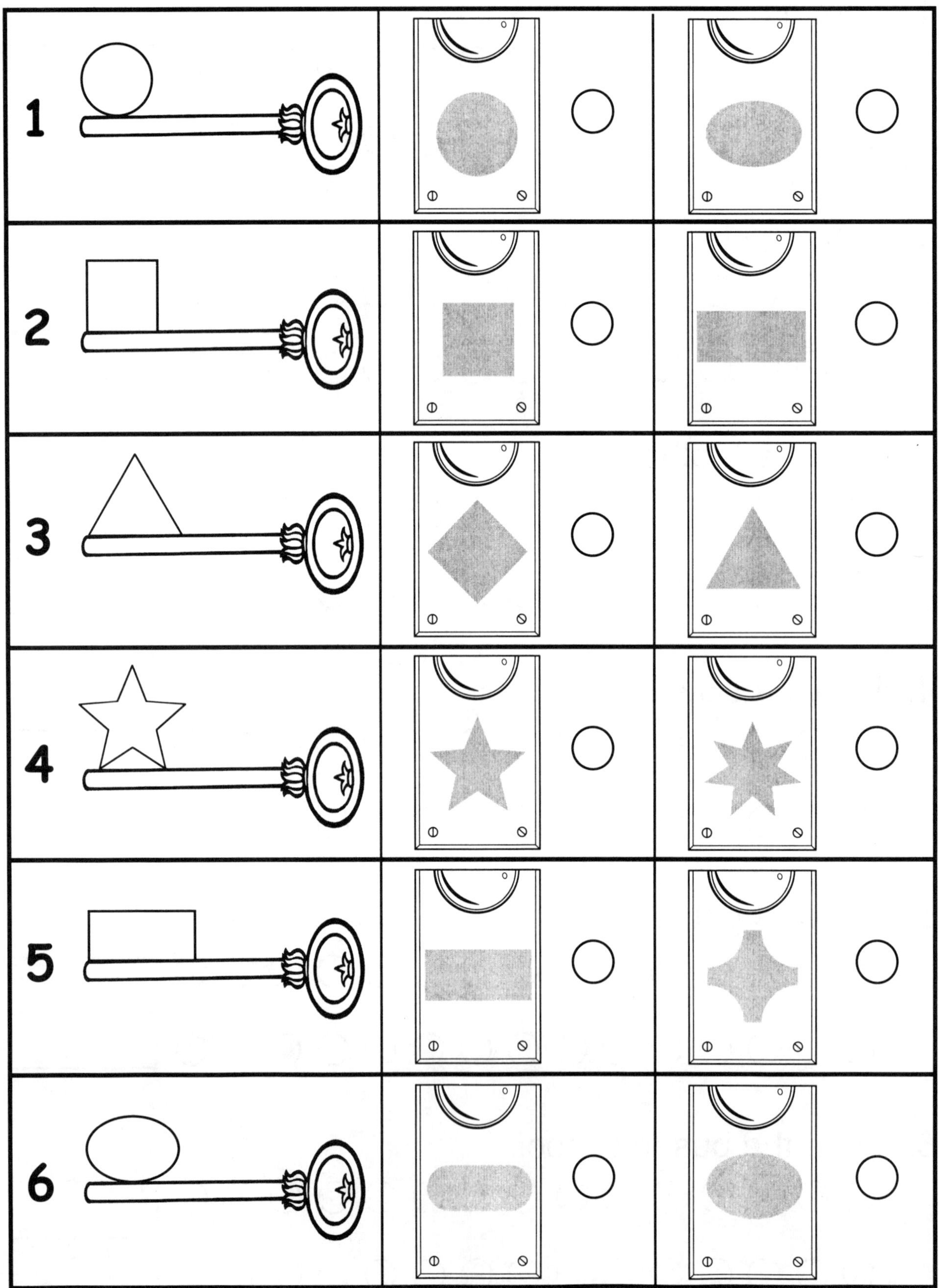

Compare the picture with Key 1 and Key 2.

Key 1	Key 2
It has fur.	It has feathers.
It has 4 legs.	It has 2 legs.
It can bark.	It can fly.

	Key 1	Key 2
Which key describes the picture?	○	○

What does the other key describe?

Use the correct letter from the key to complete each pattern.

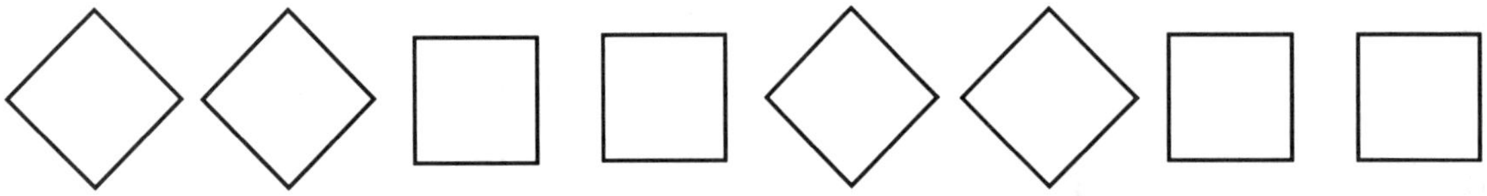

a a b b

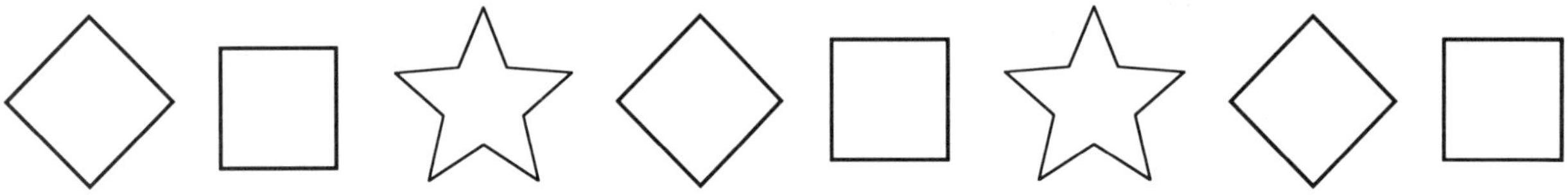

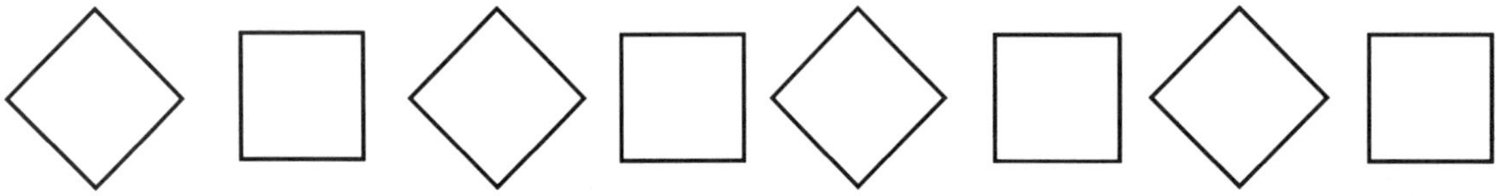

Three-In-A-Row

Cut out the pieces below to play tic-tac-toe.

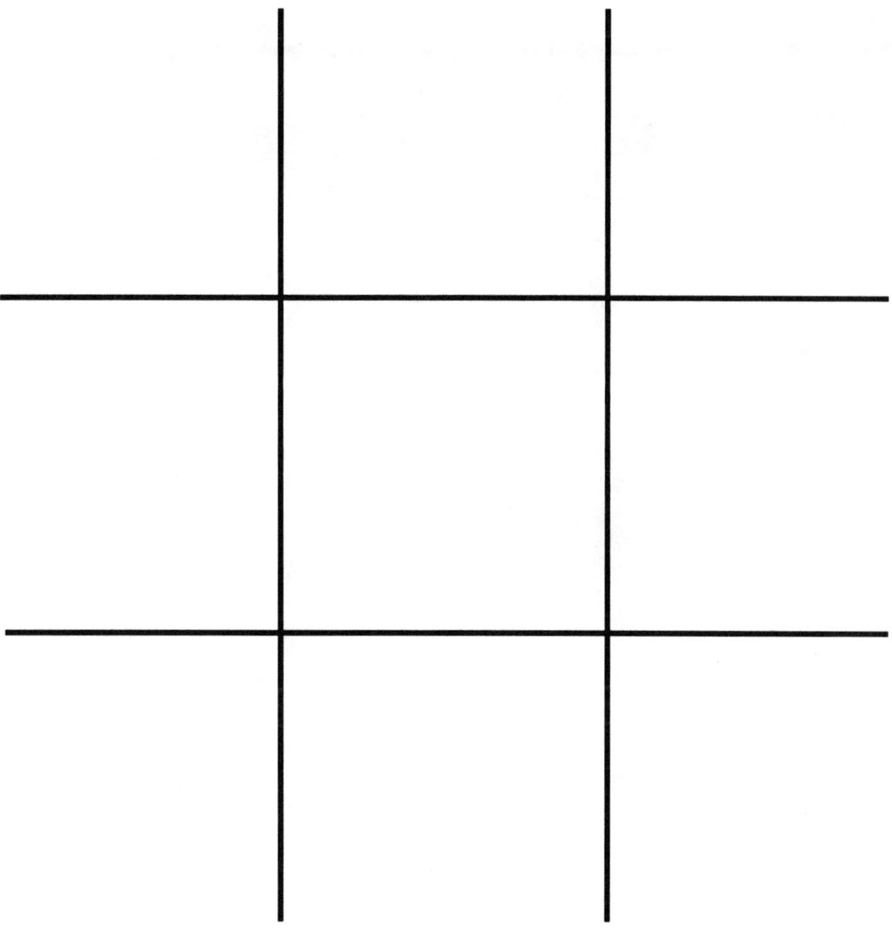

Fill in the circle to indicate the item that is next in the pattern.

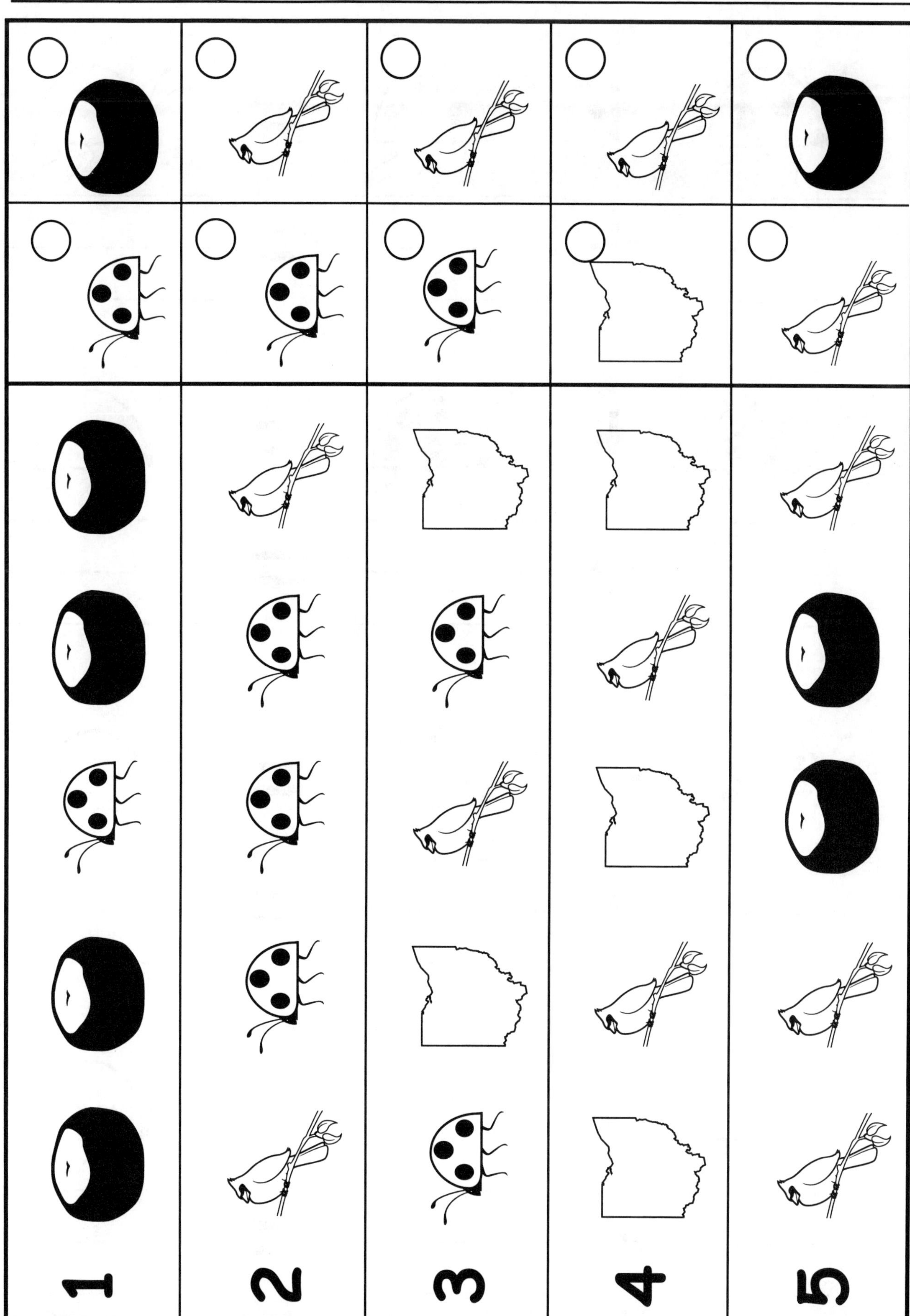

Count the number of dots on each ladybug and find the sum.

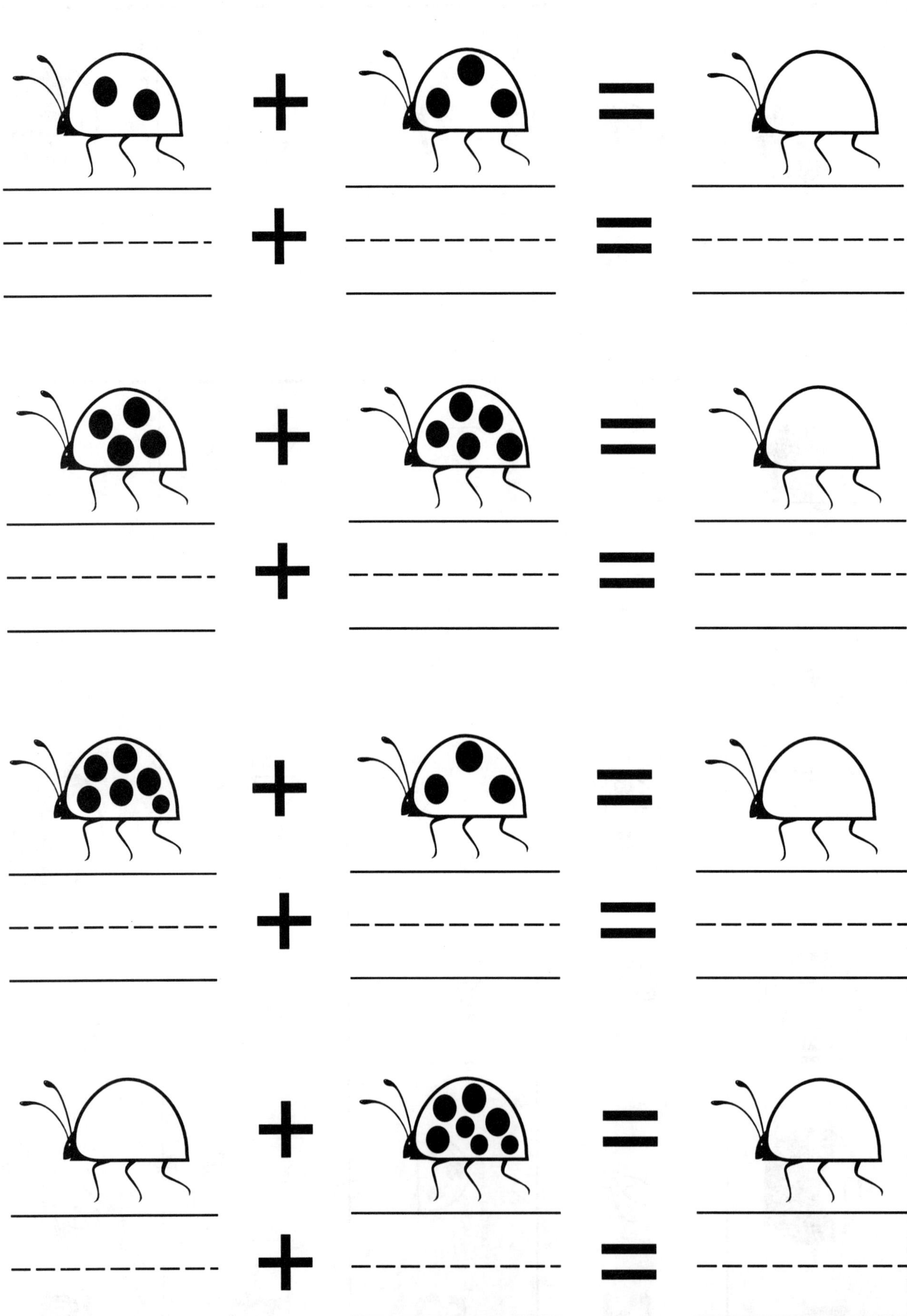

Fill in the circle to show the correct price for each item.

Fill in the circle to show whether each object is man-made or comes from nature.

Compare the Categories	**Man-Made**	**From Nature**
apple	○	○
chair	○	○
kitten	○	○
car	○	○
kite	○	○
dandelion	○	○
rocks	○	○

Color and cut out the four pictures at the bottom of the page. Glue the pictures in order from resource to product.

Draw a picture of your face in the empty box labeled "Me!" Color and cut out each of the items below. Glue the items one on top of the other in this order: globe, U.S.A., Ohio, school, Me.

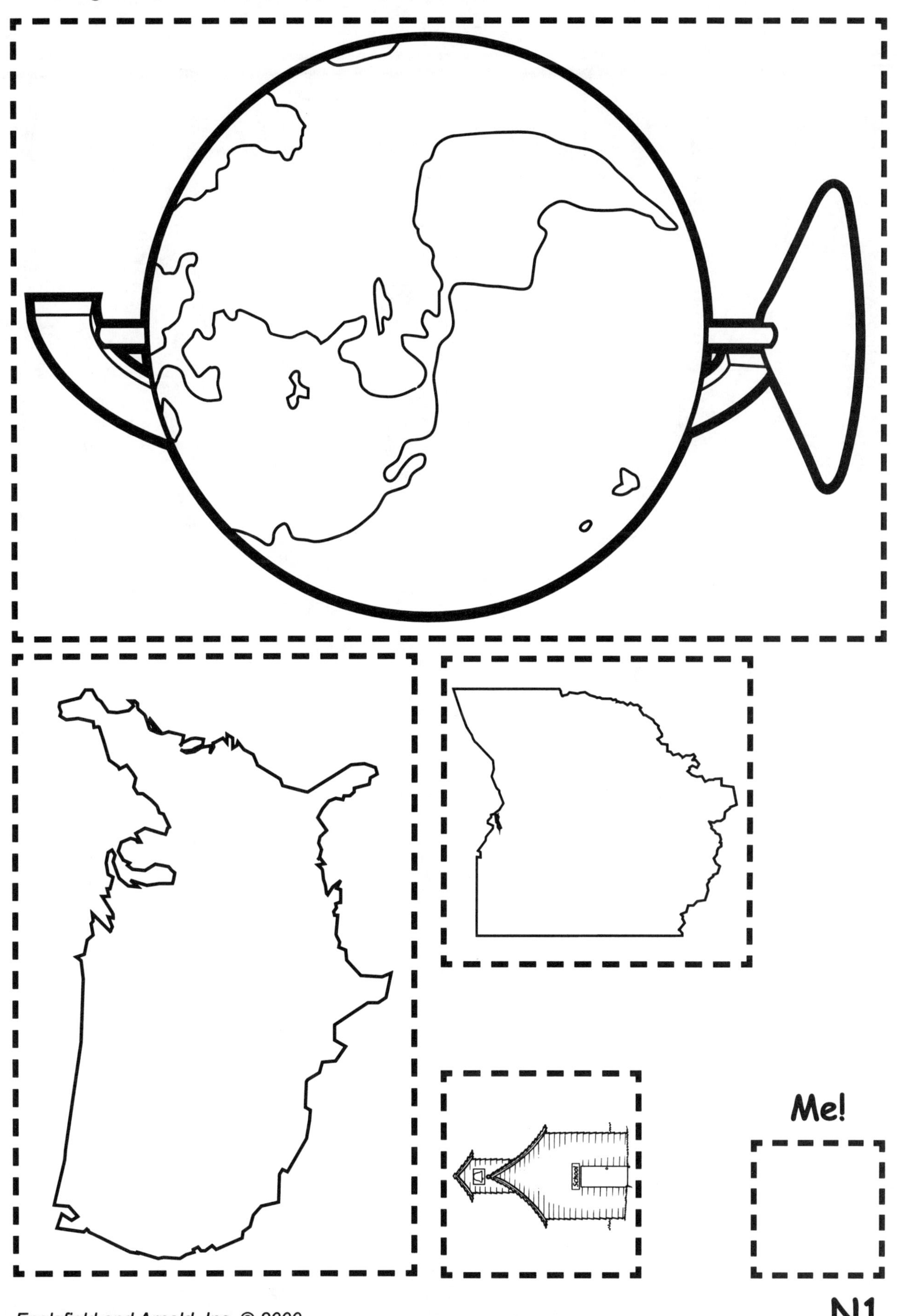

Fill in the circle if the picture shows good neighborliness.

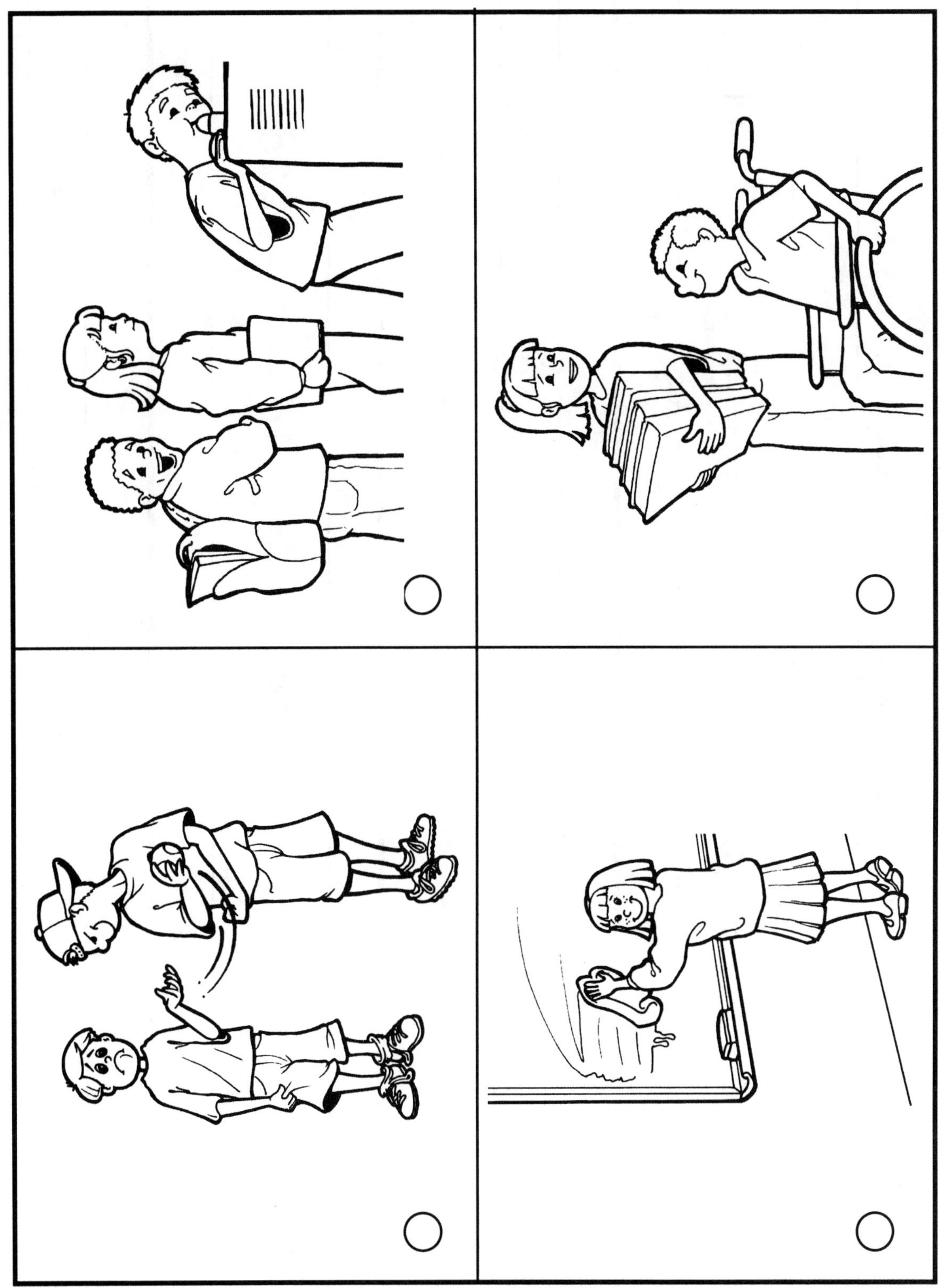

Number Neighbors

Write the numbers to complete each sequence.

1 ___ 3 ___ 5 ___ 7 ___ 9 ___ 11 ___

___ 2 ___ 4 ___ 6 ___ 8 ___ 10 ___

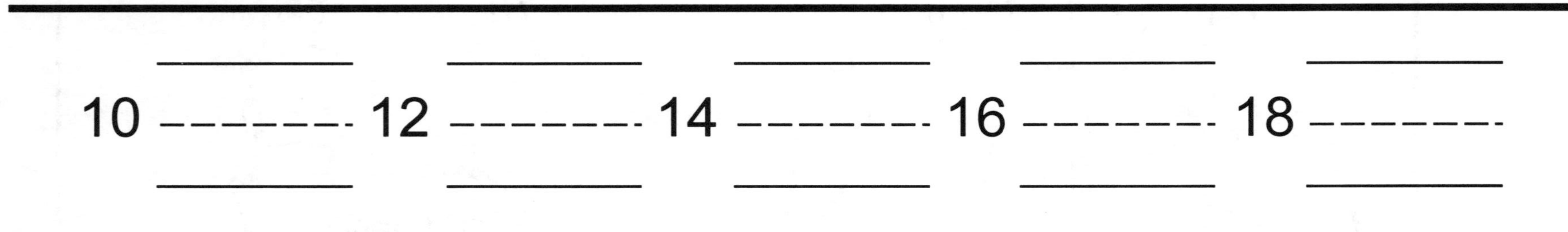

11 ___ 13 ___ 15 ___ 17 ___ 19 ___ 21

Match the digital times with the correct times on the clock faces.

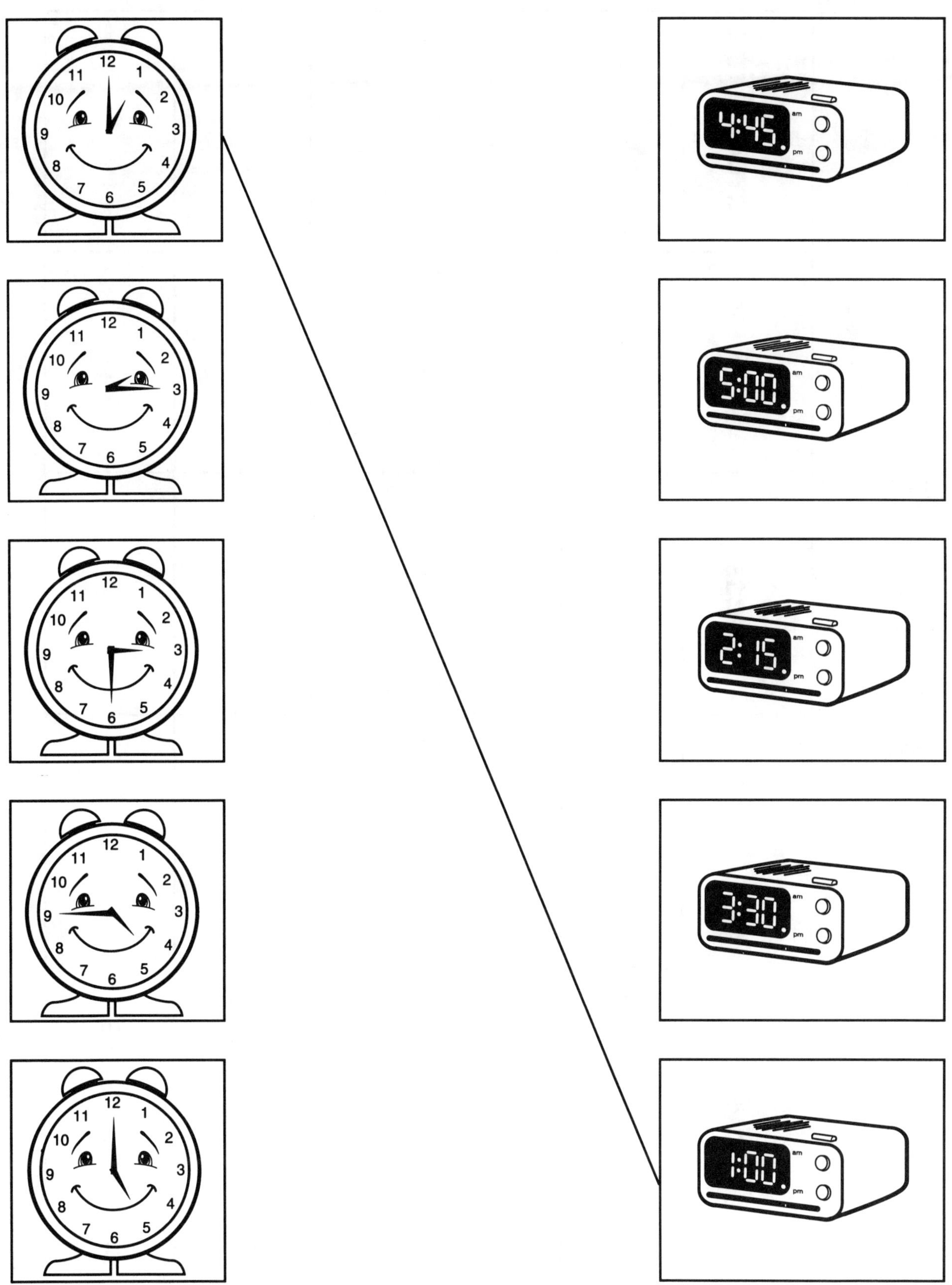

Estimate the number of seconds you could do each activity. Complete each activity and write in the actual amount of time you could do the exercise. Compare your guesses and the actual amount of time you spent.

Once Upon My Time

Activity	Guess	< = >	Actual Time
Standing on right foot			
Standing on left foot			
Standing on tip toes			
Running in place			
Jumping Jacks			

Once Upon a Time...

1. Use a red crayon to color the pepperonis.
2. Use a green crayon to color the peppers.
3. Use a yellow crayon to color the mushrooms.
4. Use a brown crayon to lightly color the crust.

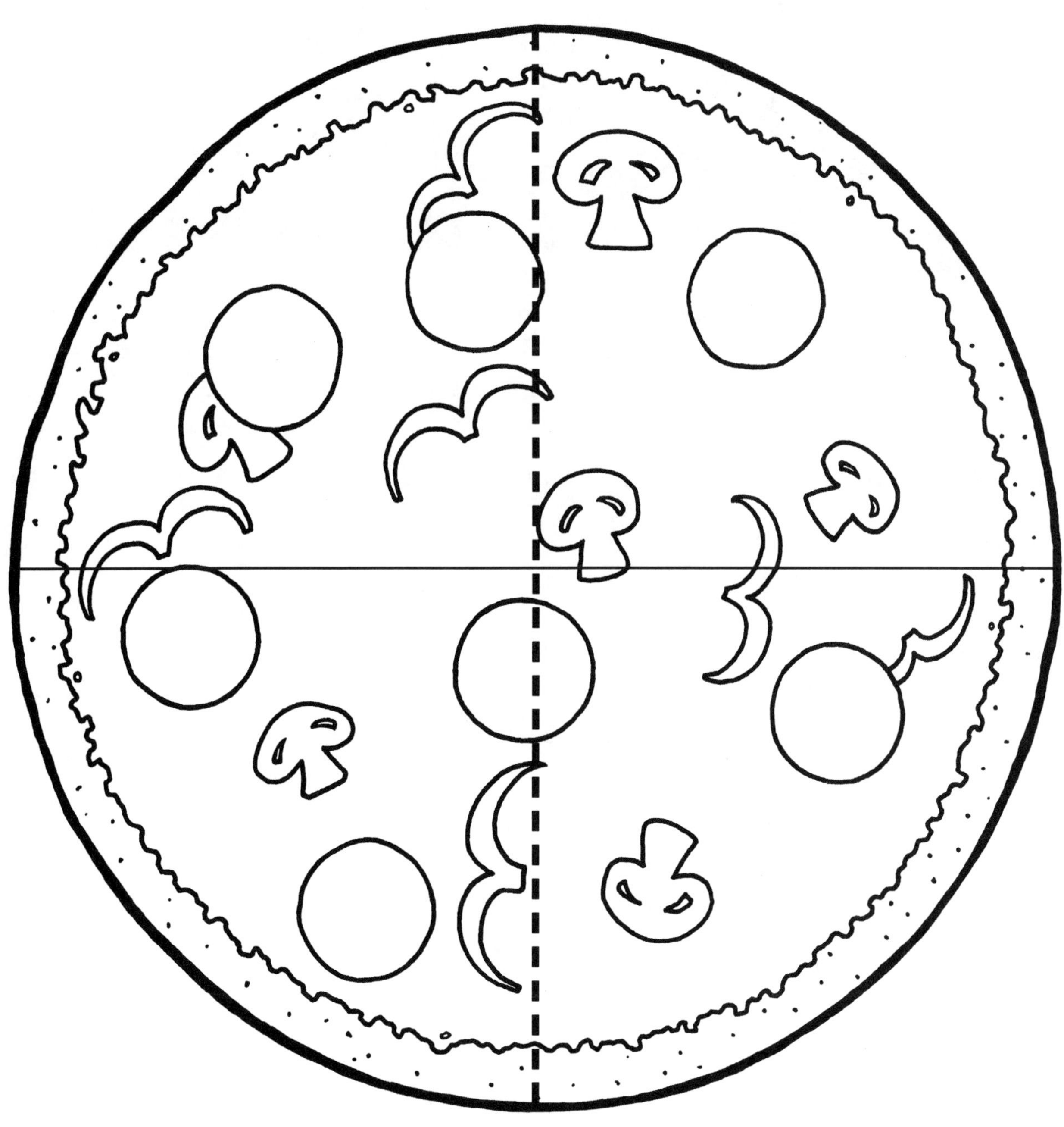

Cut out the pizza from activity P1 – cut along the outside (perimeter) of the pizza.

Fold the pizza in half along the dotted line and make a sharp crease. Re-open the folded pizza. Use a black crayon to trace along the dotted line. This line divides the pizza into two halves; each section represents 1/2. Now, fold the pizza along the solid black line. Open the pizza back up and trace the new fold. The pizza is now divided into fourths. Each piece now represents 1/4.

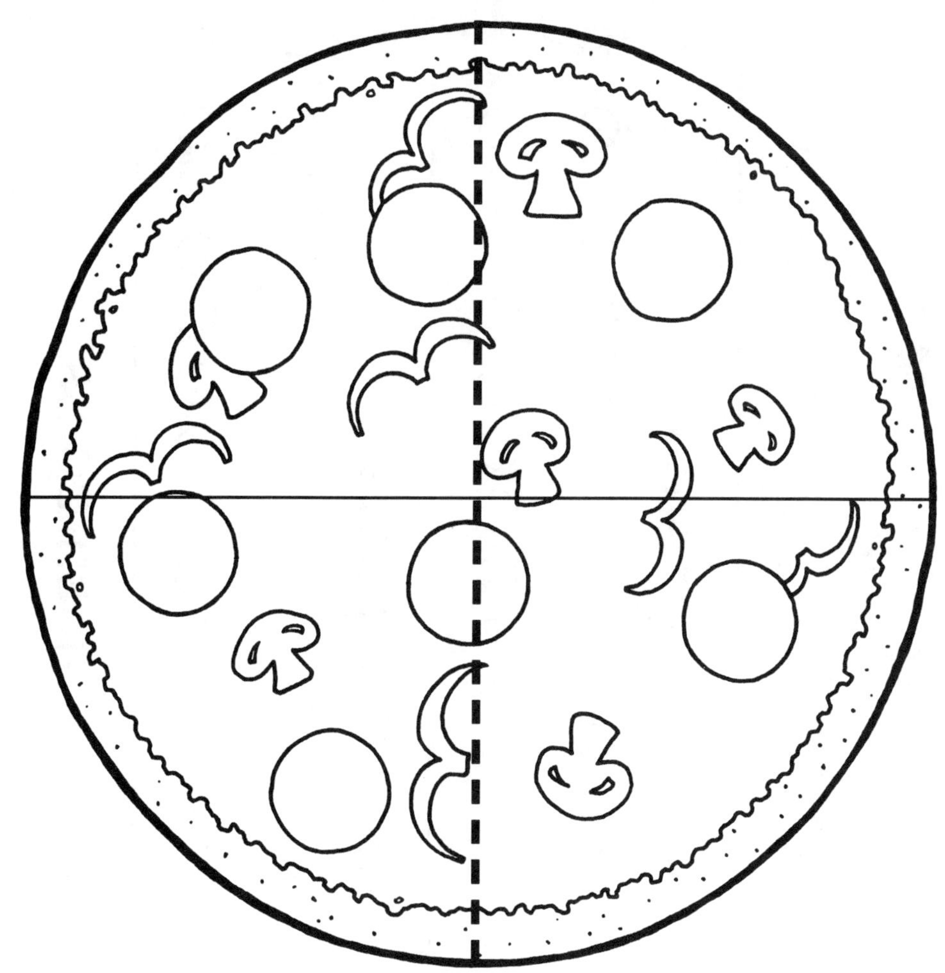

Take a class poll. Ask each student which type of pizza he or she prefers (from the four listed). As each preference is stated, students will color in one circle under the appropriate choice. Students will write in the total number for each choice on the line provided.

Pizza Poll

1. Cheese
2. Cheese and pepperoni
3. Cheese and peppers
4. Cheese and mushrooms

Notice the pattern of the Ohio Star Quilt. Cut out the triangles and squares along the dotted lines. Use the shapes to make other patterns.

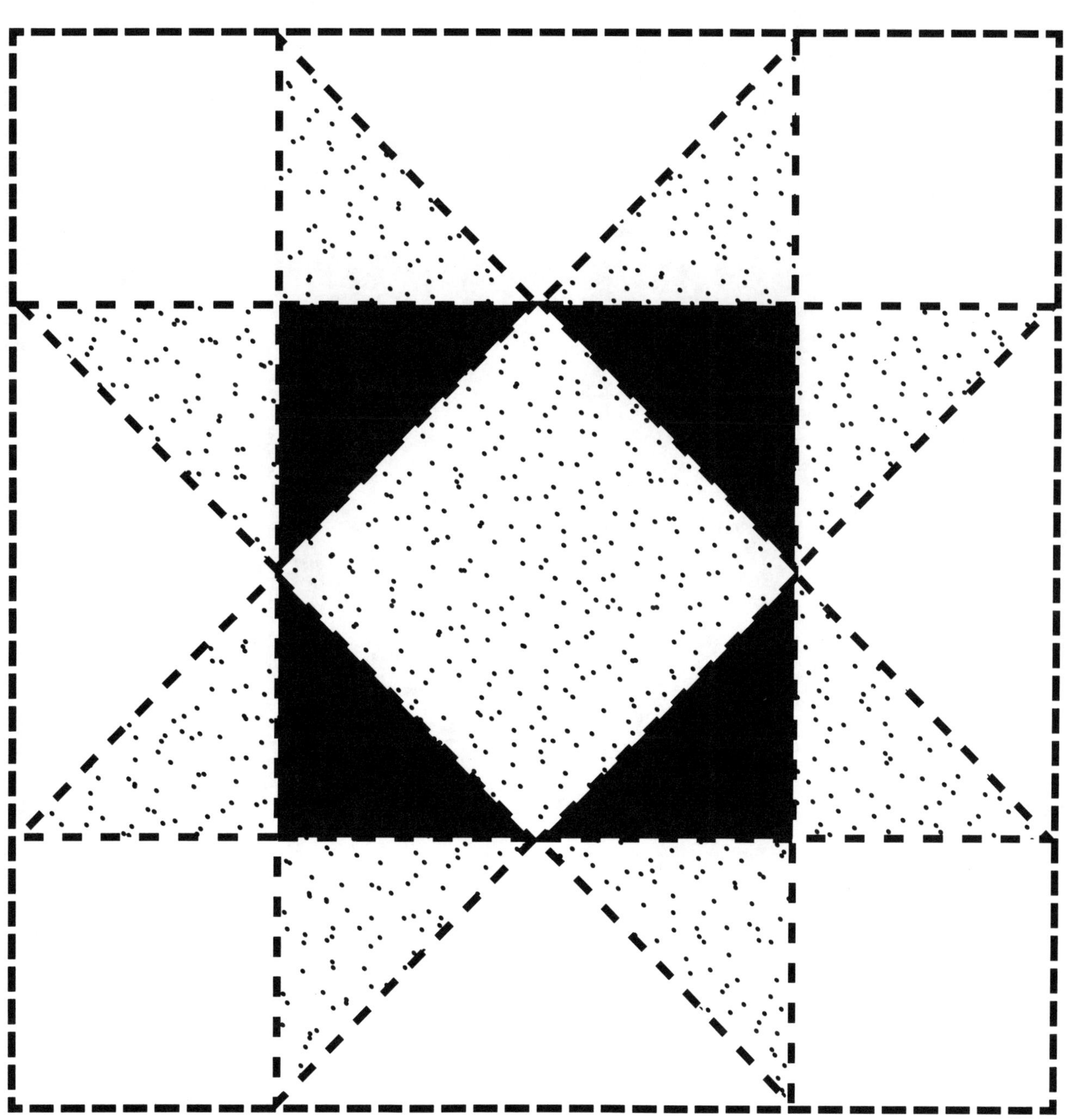

Complete the sentences.

Follow Directions

- Color the triangles red.
- Color the squares purple.
- Color the circles blue.
- Color the rectangles yellow.
- Color the ovals orange.
- Color the diamonds green.

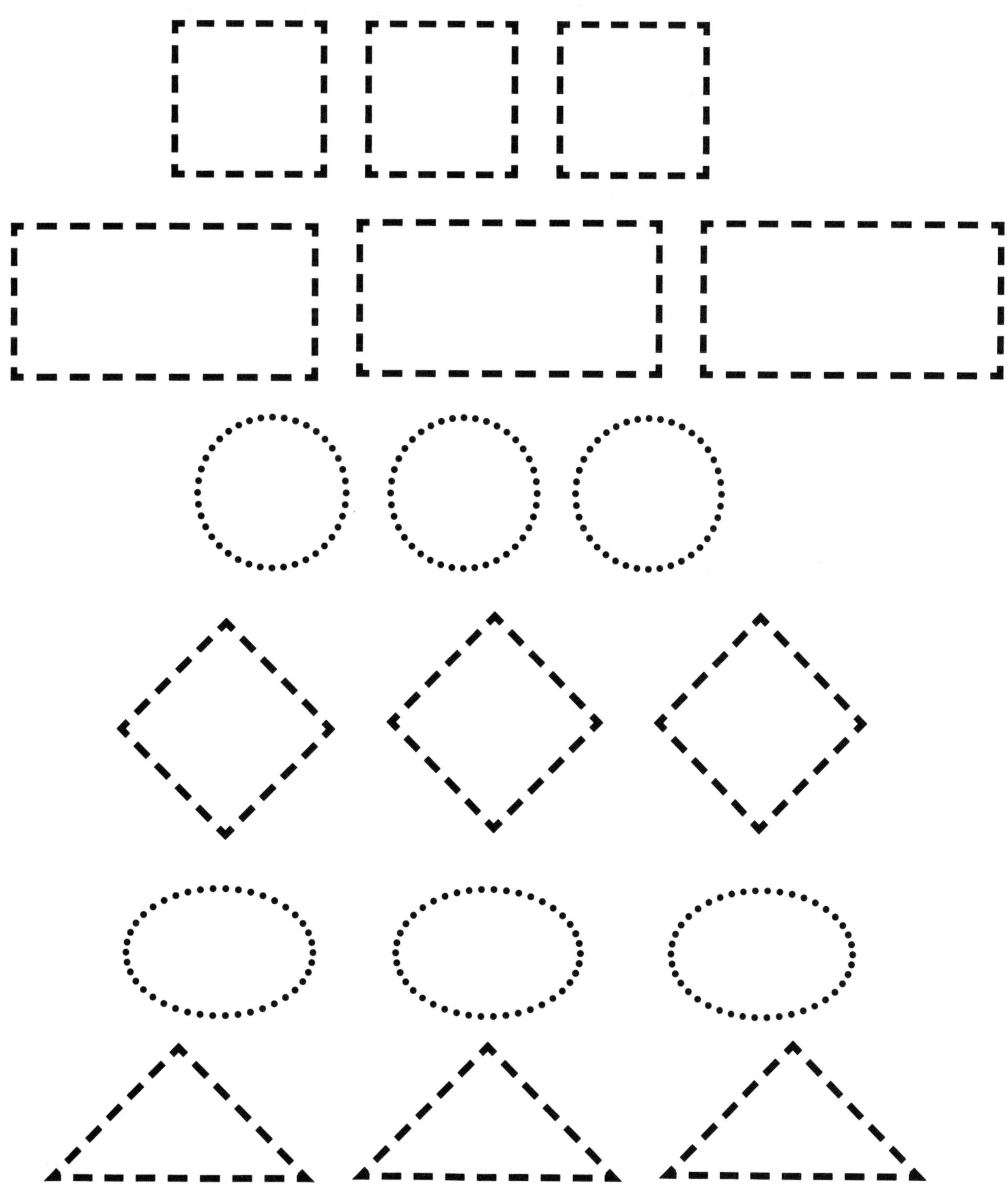

Color the number of boxes that correctly corresponds to the length of the plant root from each packet.

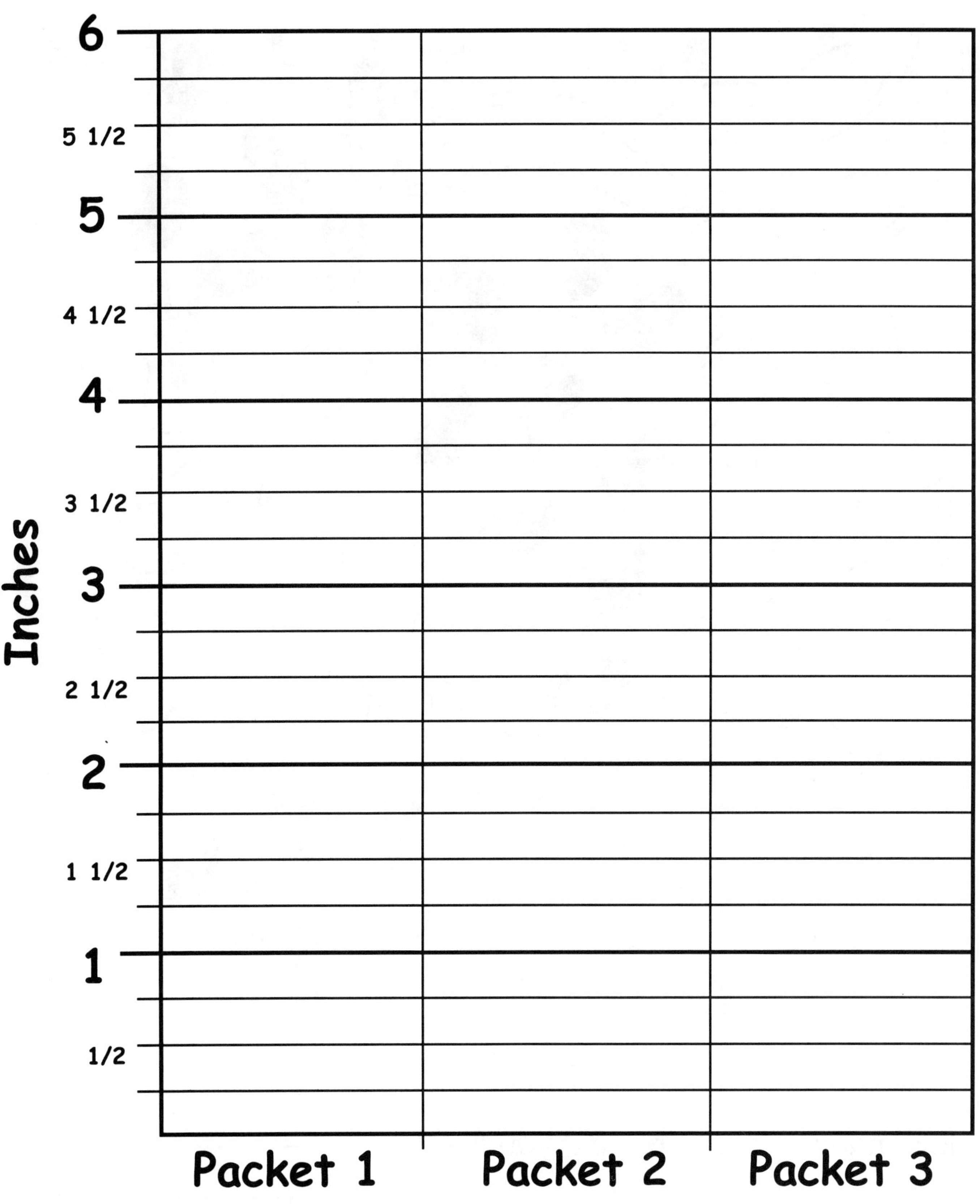

Beans in a Bunch

Draw a line around sets of three. Answer the question below.

How many sets of three did you find? ______________

Cut out each award and give to someone for a special reason.

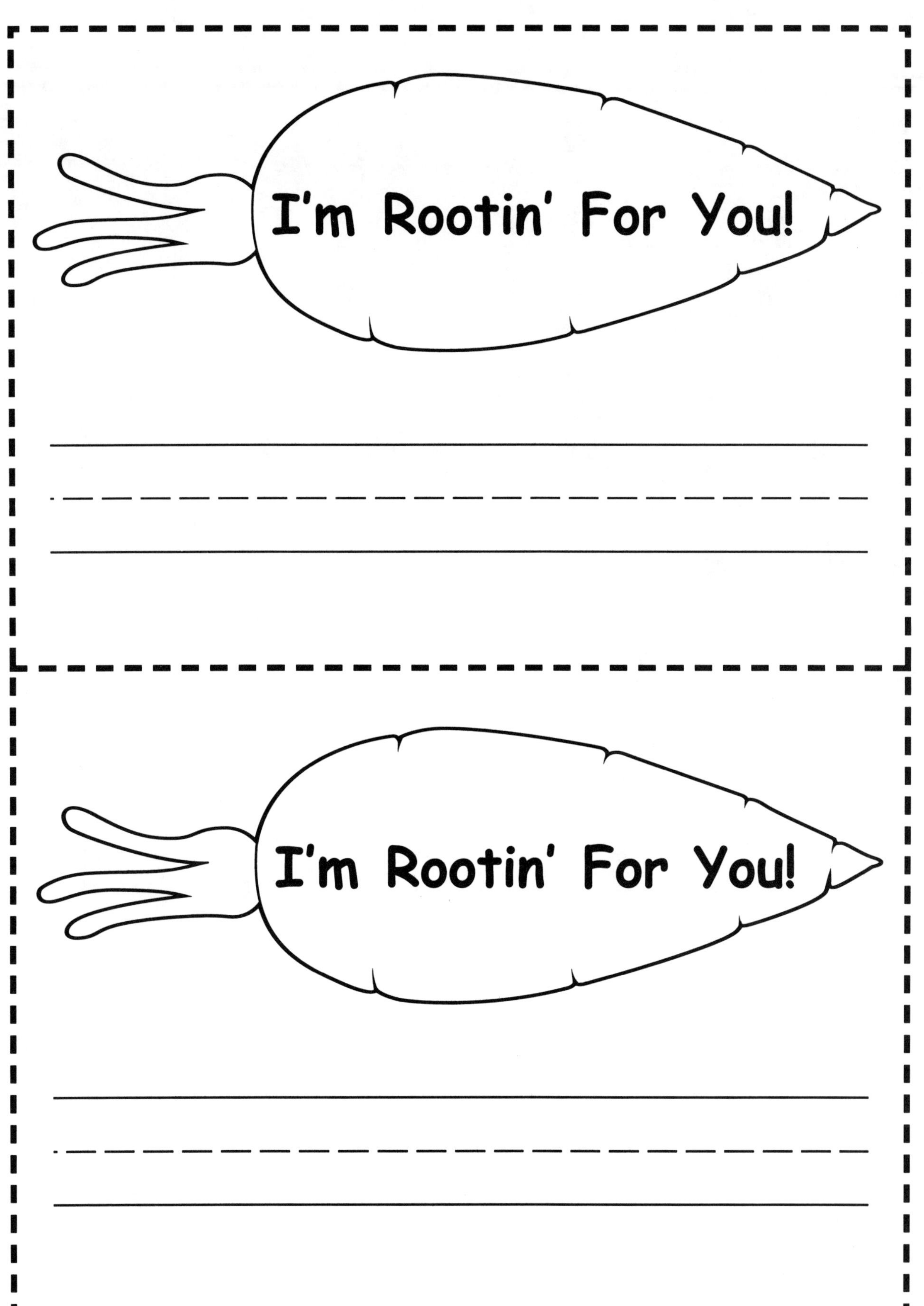

Use the five pictures below to create a rebus story.

Fill in the circle to indicate the next sign in the pattern.

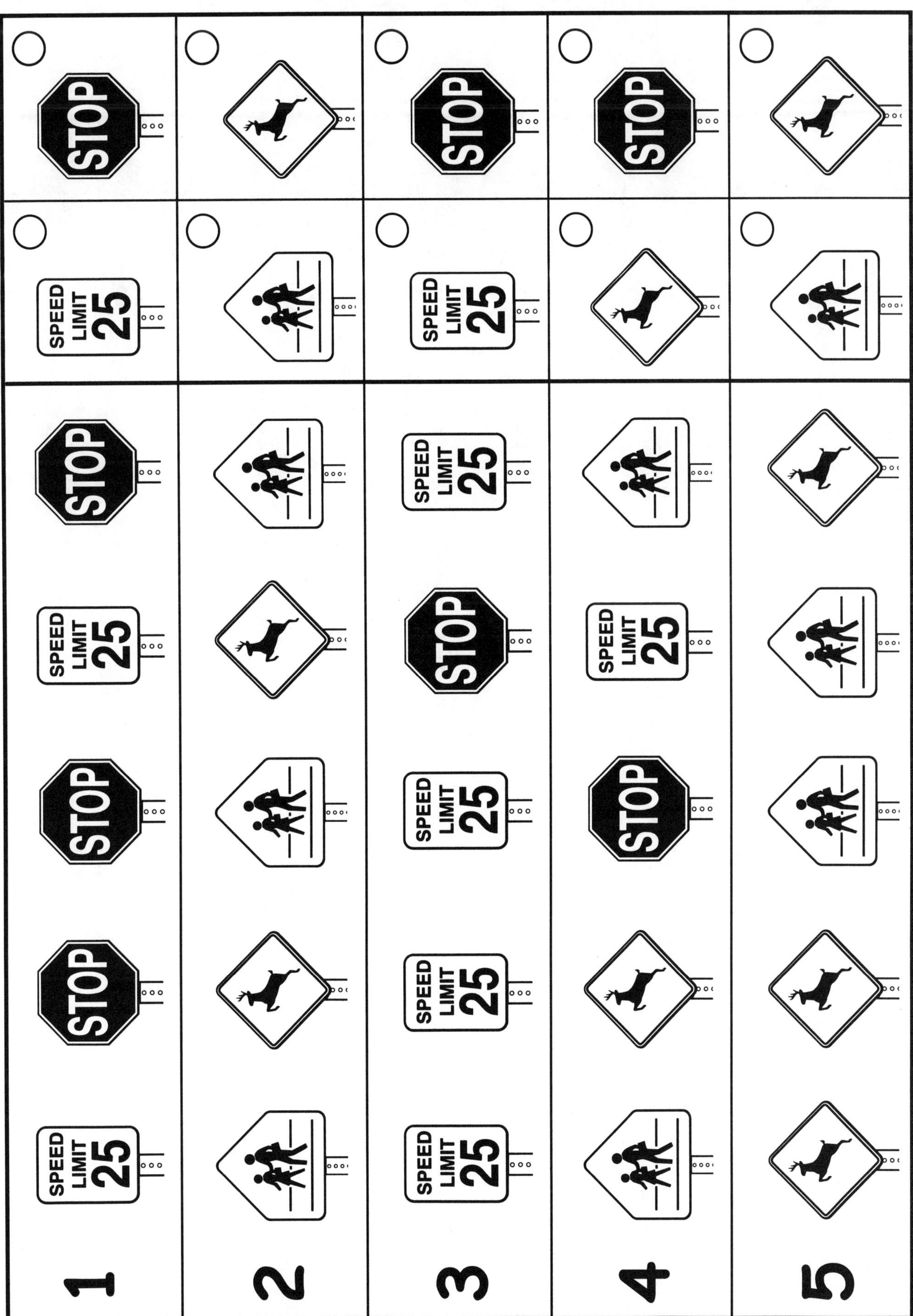

Cut out the five symbols at the bottom of the page. Paste each in the category where it belongs.

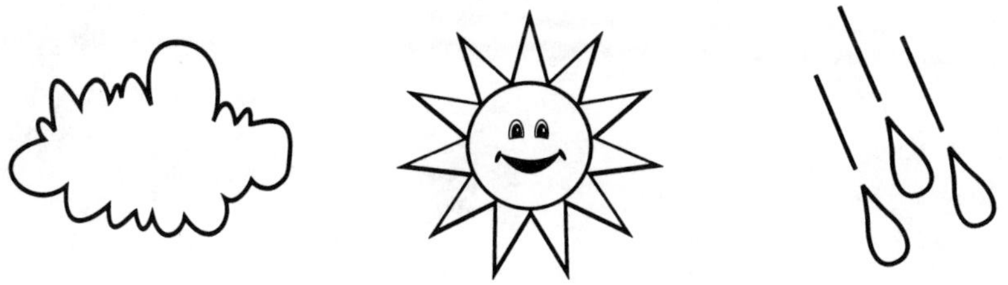	
S e n	
6 2 8	
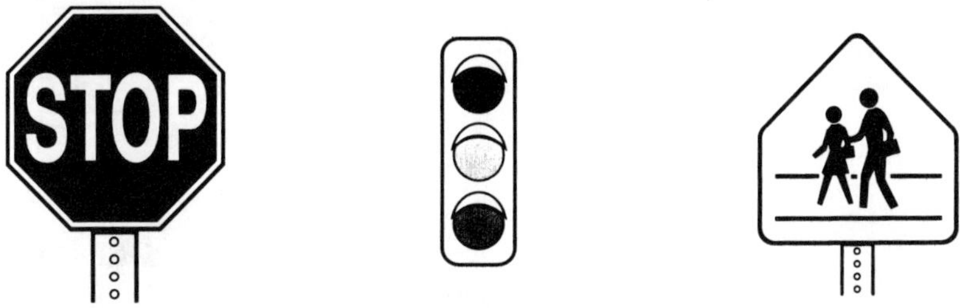 STOP	
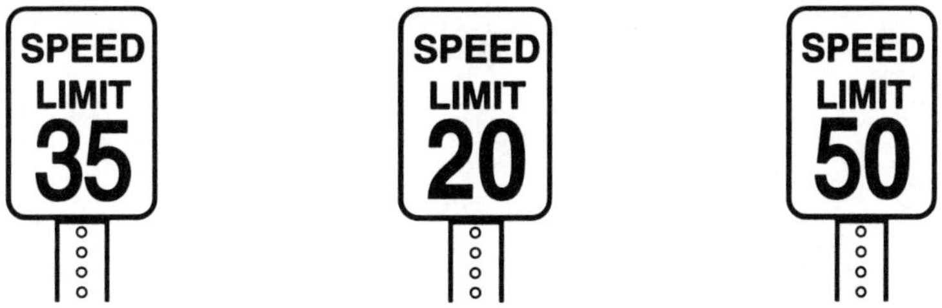 SPEED LIMIT 35 SPEED LIMIT 20 SPEED LIMIT 50	

SPEED LIMIT 40
A
9

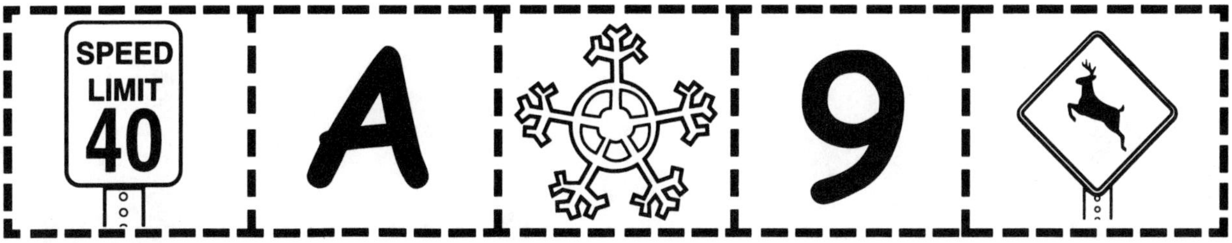

Write a tale on the lion's tail.

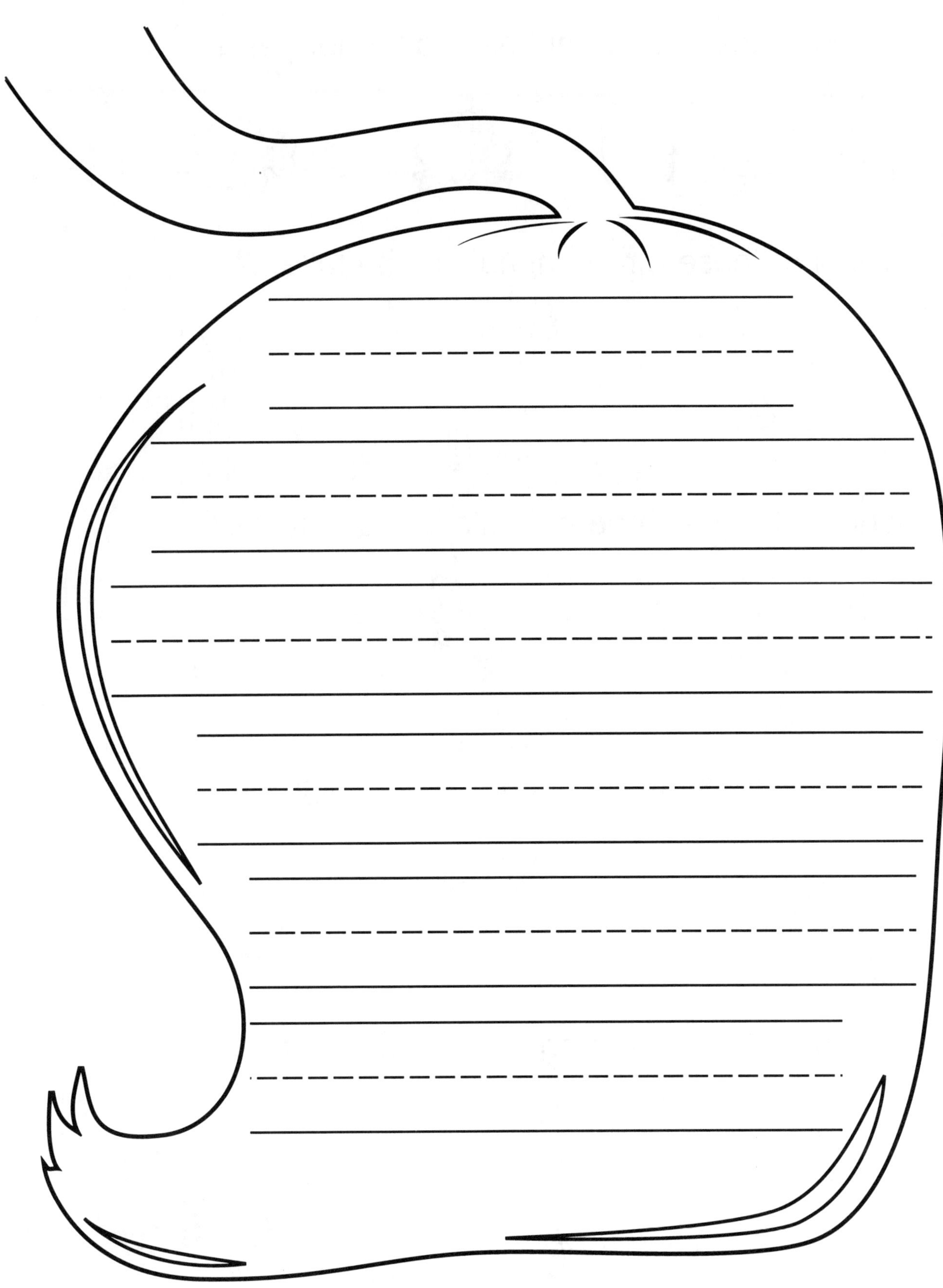

Color the correct answer.

1. Which of these three animals is the longest?

2. Which of these three animals is the tallest?

3. Which of these three animals is the smallest?

4. Which of these three animals is the biggest?

5. Which of these three animals is the shortest?

Fill in the correct circle to identify the symbol that correctly compares the set in the left column to the set in the right column.

	< ○ > ○ = ○	
	< ○ > ○ = ○	
	< ○ > ○ = ○	
	< ○ > ○ = ○	

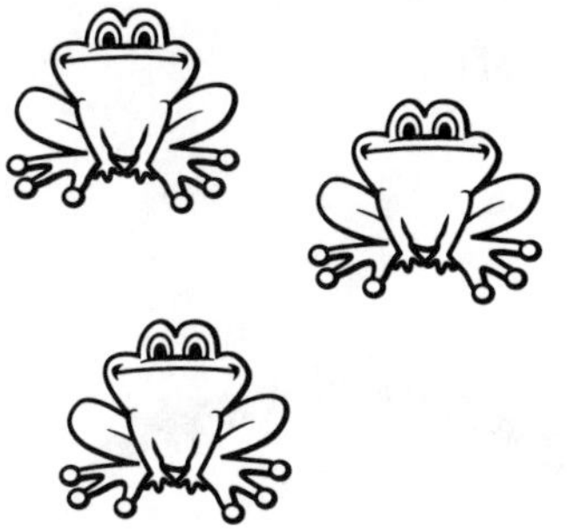

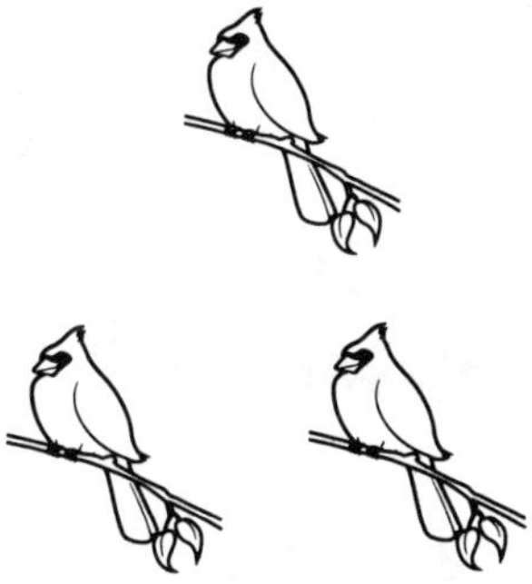

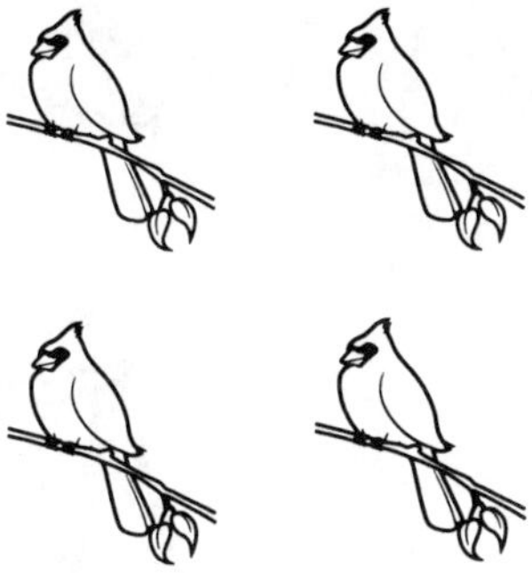

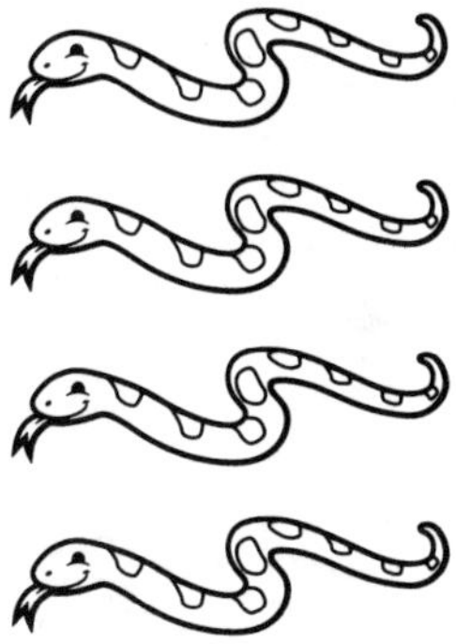

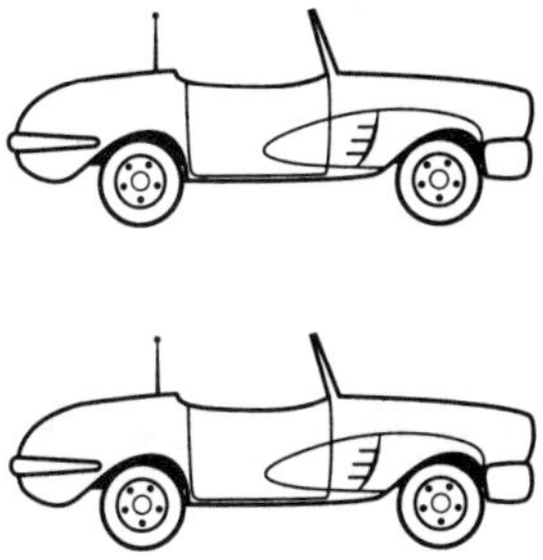

Use a pencil to guide the rabbit through the park.

1. The rabbit hops through the tunnel.
2. The rabbit runs around the tree.
3. The rabbit hops under the swingset.
4. The rabbit climbs up the slide ladder.
5. The rabbit goes down the slide.
6. The rabbit hops across the sandbox and finds his carrot.

Recognize opposite words. Look at the words in the left column. Fill in the circles to identify opposite word partners.

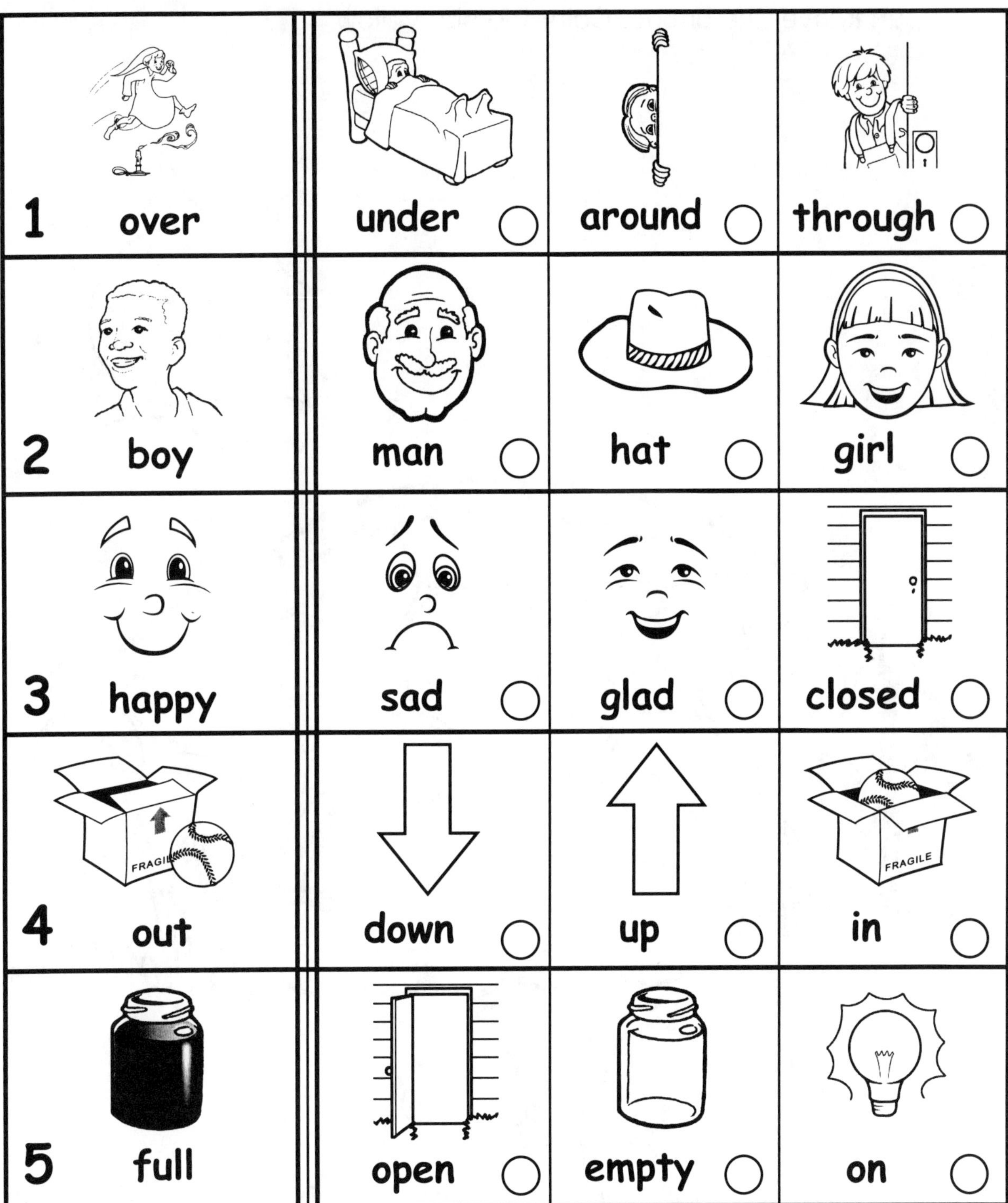

1 over	under ○	around ○	through ○
2 boy	man ○	hat ○	girl ○
3 happy	sad ○	glad ○	closed ○
4 out	down ○	up ○	in ○
5 full	open ○	empty ○	on ○

Follow Directions

- The fish swims through the river. Color the fish orange.
- The river is under the bridge. Color the river blue.
- The cattails are around the river. Color the cattails green.
- The bridge is over the river. Color the bridge brown.
- The sun is over the bridge. Color the sun yellow.

Match the word equations to the correct number equations.

---

four plus one equals five	10 - 3 = 7
three minus two equals one	5 + 4 = 9
ten minus three equals seven	9 - 3 = 6
six plus two equals eight	3 - 2 = 1
five plus four equals nine	4 + 1 = 5
nine minus three equals six	6 + 2 = 8

Complete each sentence.

1. I rode my bike to the ________________.
   noun

2. My mom made ________________ for the family.
   noun

3. The ________________ balloon floated in the air.
   adjective

4. The ________________ ________________.
   noun verb

Fill in the circle to identify the punctuation mark that completes each sentence.

	.	?	!
1. We won the game	○	○	○
2. Do you ride the bus to school	○	○	○
3. I went fishing on Saturday	○	○	○
4. Are you going to the library today	○	○	○

Fill in the circle(s) to identify the correct answer choice(s).	whale	seal	goldfish
I live in water.	○	○	○
I can live in a small bowl.	○	○	○
I cannot live in a small bowl.	○	○	○
I use my fins as feet.	○	○	○
I do not use my fins as feet.	○	○	○

Cut out each sentence below. Paste the parts of each sentence that answer "who," "what," or "where" in the correct columns.

Who	What	Where

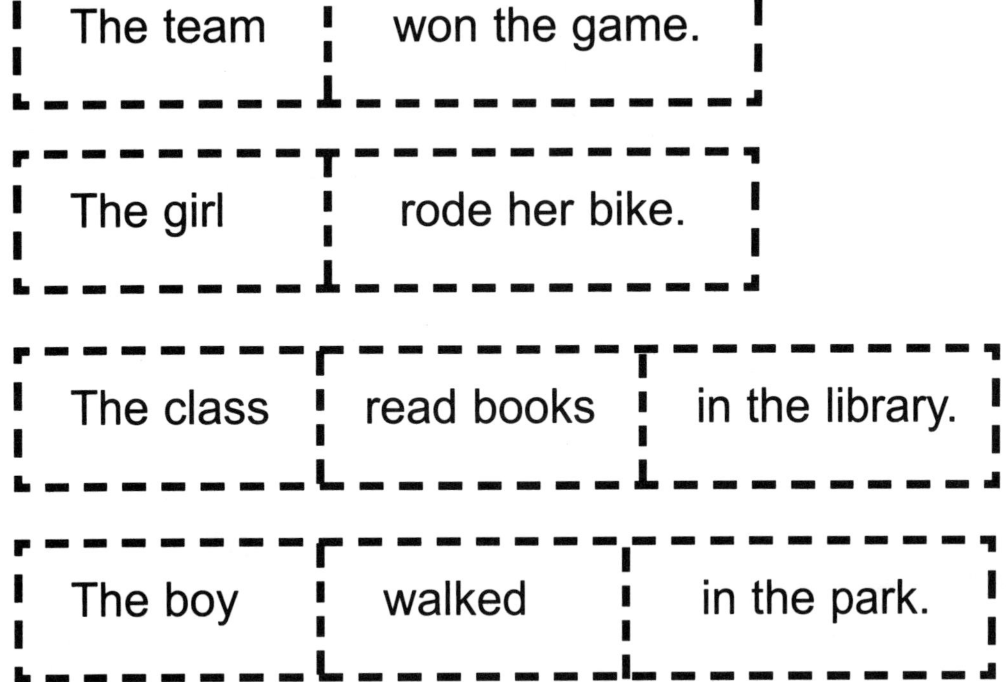

Cut along the dotted lines and fold along the solid line to create a table tent.

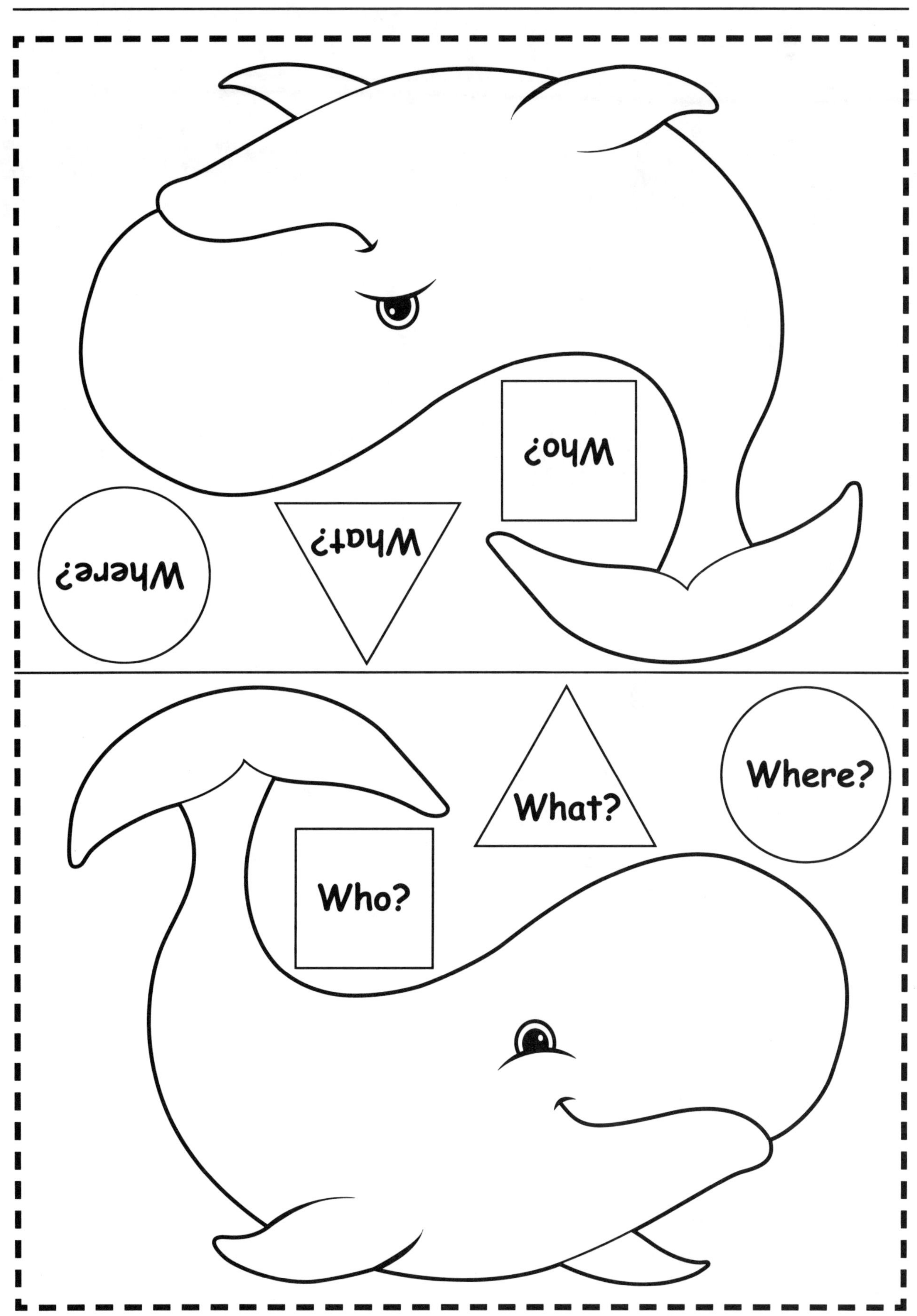

Fill in the circles to identify living things.

Study the fishbowls and write three things that are the same.

1

2

3

Cut out and paste the measuring instruments below to solve the following riddles.

I can be used to measure flour for making bread. What am I?	
I can be used to measure inches and centimeters. What am I?	
I can be used to check the temperature. What am I?	
I can be used to time a race. What am I?	

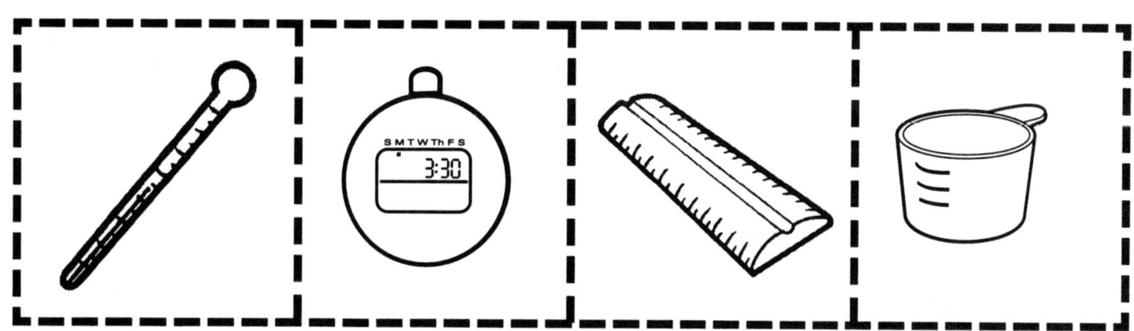

Draw a line connecting the animal to its habitat.

You have been left to care for the neighbor's pets and special instructions are given for you to buy a certain number of items each day. Fill in a circle to indicate the correct price for each item.

Item		
10¢	11¢ ○	10¢ ○
25¢	22¢ ○	25¢ ○
15¢	15¢ ○	16¢ ○
20¢	30¢ ○	20¢ ○
5¢	5¢ ○	4¢ ○

Carefully cut along the dotted lines. Fold along the solid lines to create a variety of animals using different heads, bodies and feet.

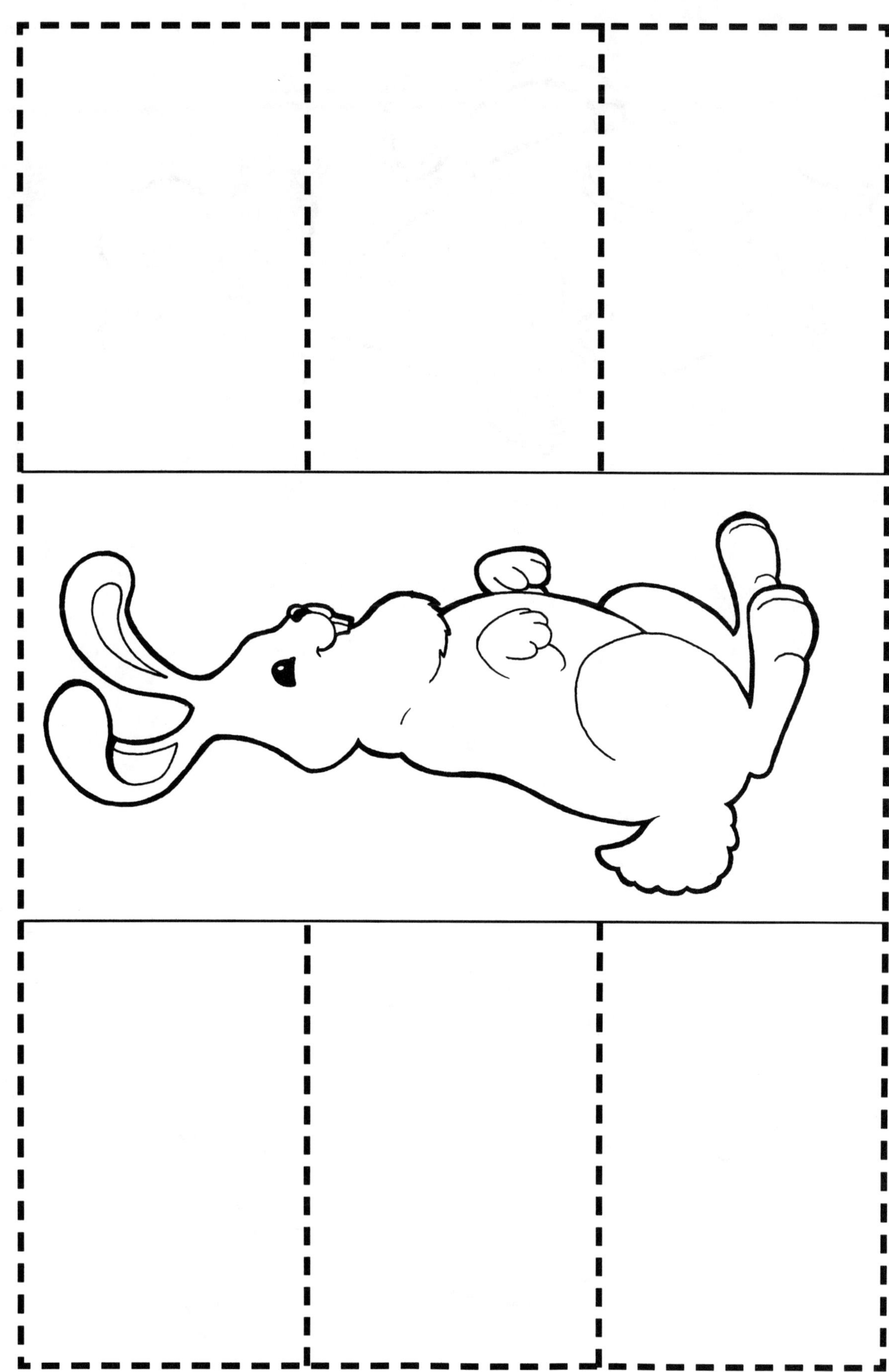